Our United States of America

STUDENT WORKBOOK AND ANSWER KEY

By CHC Staff with Nancy Nicholson

to accompany

Our United States of America

by Oliver Corrigan

Catholic Heritage Curricula
1-800-490-7713   www.chcweb.com

Web Links and Video Clips: Parental supervision is strongly advised when your child is visiting recommended website links. At the time of this printing these links contained helpful information that was age-appropriate. Be advised that good links can change frequently, becoming inappropriate or no longer available. Because of this, please visit recommended web links beforehand and supervise student during his online visit. Use of an ad-blocker when browsing links is also highly recommended.

ISBN: 978-0-9883797-4-9

© 2013 Catholic Heritage Curricula
This book is under copyright. All rights reserved. No part of this book may be reproduced in any form by any means—electronic, mechanical, or graphic—without prior written permission. Thank you for honoring copyright law.

Cover and Interior Design: RoseMary Johnson

For more information:
Catholic Heritage Curricula
www.chcweb.com

Maps credit: www.d-maps.com

Cover image credits: iStockphoto/Thinkstock.com; Bridgeman Art Library/Immaculate Conception, c.1575 (oil on canvas), Barocci or Baroccio, Federico Fiori (c.1535-1612)/Galleria Nazionale delle Marche, Urbino, Italy/Alinari; The Granger Collection, New York; Wikimedia Commons Public Domain; "The Gathering" by Sr. M. Julius Hausmann and Sr. M. Lurana Neely, photographed by Bob Borton/Fire and Ice Imagery and provided courtesy of the Archives of the Sisters of the Blessed Sacrament. Photo credit pg. 126: The Driver Family. Back cover image credit: The Granger Collection, New York.

Printed by Sheridan Books
Chelsea, Michigan
May 2021

Table of Contents

INTRODUCTION	1
NORTHEASTERN REGION:	
New England	7
Mid-Atlantic	25
MIDWESTERN REGION:	
East North-Central	31
West North-Central	40
SOUTHERN REGION:	
South Atlantic	47
East & West South-Central	57
WESTERN REGION:	
Mountain	67
Pacific	72
LEARNING ABOUT MY STATE	83
ANSWER KEY	127

Teacher's Note

This **Student Workbook** provides exercises, enrichment activities, reviews and tests, and a complete answer key to accompany the text *Our United States of America: Catholic Social Studies*. The **Student Text** is designed to be completed in 27 weeks, allowing the student nine weeks to devote to studying his own state. The step-by-step, nine-week guide found in the **Student Workbook** guides the student in researching and writing about the history, geography, and culture of his state. Together, the text and workbook of *Our United States of America: Catholic Social Studies* constitute a complete, 36-week program.

Text and Workbook may be purchased from Catholic Heritage Curricula at *www.chcweb.com*. A daily lesson plan for scheduling *Our United States of America: Catholic Social Studies* can be found in *CHC Lesson Plans for Fourth Grade* and *Our United States of America Daily Lesson Plans*, also available at *www.chcweb.com*.

Introduction

Tricks to Finding Clues as We Read

To **study** something means to carefully examine it, to "look it over" and think about what you see.

If you were to study a rose, you might see flower petals, a stem, and leaves. With more study, you might notice different colors in the petals. You might sniff the rose and smell a beautiful perfume, and notice thorns on the stem. After thinking about all these things, you might be able to tell someone not only about the pretty smell and colors, but also to beware of sharp thorns!

There are also ways to study textbooks, "tricks" that will help you learn and remember, tricks that will make it so you can share with others the surprising things that you have learned.

The first trick is to read every single thing on the page. Another trick is bolding of "clue words." **Bolded** words are darker, like **this**. When we see a word in bold, it gives us a clue that it's a very important word to learn.

Yet another trick is *italicizing* of a word, like *this*.

Paying special attention to bold or italicized words makes it easier to understand what we read. Discovering these clue words also helps us to study, learn, and remember.

Directions: Turn to the "Introduction" on pages 1-9 in the text and look for clues! Circle the correct answers.

1. The first two bolded words tell us about the study of people's culture. Which two words are bolded?

   a. ancient centuries   b. ancient cultures   c. social studies

2. Count all the **bold** words in the "Introduction." (*Do not count the words in topic headings.*) How many words are in bold?

   a. 15   b. 20   c. 25

More Tricks to Finding Clues

You know that words in *italics* are slanted, like *this* to tell us that the words are important. Sometimes italicized words are also bolded, like ***this***.

Sidebars like this one about Christopher Columbus also point to important information.

Sidebars are like boxes on the page. They add interesting or useful information that tells a little more about the subject.

Did You Know?

Christopher Columbus

Christopher Columbus discovered America in 1492.

In your *Our United States* text, sidebars can be found at the bottom or top of the page. Sometimes they will even fill the whole page!

Paying special attention to clue words and information in side bars, and reading the definitions included in the text, makes it easier to understand what we read. Discovering these clue words also helps us to study, learn, and remember.

1. The sidebar on this page tells about a person. Write the name of the person, below.

   ....

2. Look through the "Introduction" to find the first four words that are not bolded, but are in *italics.* (These four words are all found in the same sentence.) Write the four words below.

   ....
   ....

3. The four italicized words are the names of three

   a. ships   b. countries   c. people

Introduction

Finding More Clues

Directions: Turn to the "Introduction" and look for clues! Circle the correct answers. *Be sure to use your clue-finding tricks!*

1. Social studies is

    a. the study of a people's culture, the way they live, work, play, and celebrate

    b. centuries long past

    c. the study of the Catholic Church

2. People who study ancient cultures and look for clues about them are called

    a. archaeologists   b. ancient peoples   c. hide and seekers

3. Immigrants are people who

    a. are great-grandparents   b. traveled from another country to a new land

4. The American colonies were

    a. large settlements started by people from other countries, that belonged to another country

    b. large groups of knees

    c. English and Dutch people who explored here long ago

5. An economy is

    a. the making, buying, and selling goods, which create jobs

    b. a type of natural resource

    c. a type of transportation

Introduction

6. Agriculture is another word for

   a. fishingb. farmingc. basketball

7. Government is

   a. things that are found in the water or soil

   b. ways to travel from place to place

   c. a system of leaders, laws, and rules by which a nation lives

8. Another word for "clues" to what we study and why things happen is

   a. mysteryb. evidencec. understand

Why Did Americans Want a New Government?

Directions: Read "America's System of Government." Then answer the questions. Be sure to use your tricks for finding clues!

1. A *system of government* is the way a country is ....

2. A *colony* is a land that doesn't "belong" to itself, but belongs to another ....

3. People who live in colonies are called ....

4. The British forced Americans to follow unfair rules or laws. Name at least two of the unfair laws or rules that the British made Americans follow.

   ....
   ....
   ....
   ....
   ....

5. Americans revolted against British rule. This revolt turned into what war?

   ....

6. The Declaration of Independence was written to tell the British what?

   ....
   ....
   ....

America's System of Government

When Americans won their freedom from the British, they created a new system of government. This new system allowed Americans to vote, to choose their leaders.

Directions: Read "America's System of Government." Then answer the questions about this new system of government. Be sure to use your tricks for finding clues!

1. Independence Day is a day to celebrate what?
   ....

2. On what day do Americans celebrate their independence?
   ....

3. What is the name of America's set of laws that rule the nation?
   ....

4. Our form of government is divided into three "branches." The executive branch is led
   a. by Congress   b. by the president   c. by senators   d. by votes

5. The legislative branch of our government is called
   a. the president   b. senators   c. Congress   d. votes

6. Congress is made up of two parts called ....
   ....

7. The judicial branch of government is made up of the ....
   of the Supreme .... When there is a disagreement about a law, this court decides whether or not the law agrees with the Constitution.

8. The federal government is the government of our whole
   a. nation   b. state   c. city

6   Introduction

Northeastern Region

NEW ENGLAND

Lessons Alive!

Teacher's Note: "Lessons Alive!" activities animate and reinforce "text learning" through real-life, hands-on experience. "Lessons Alive!" appears at the beginning of each new region to allow time for selecting activities and gathering any materials necessary for chosen enrichment lessons.

Connecticut

- Connecticut's contribution to The Great Compromise pleased both strong and weak states. Write a constitution for your family that will please everyone in your family, parents and children alike. Be prepared to make some compromises!
- What kind of activities are the Knights of Columbus involved in, in your parish and community? Can you watch or participate in some of their activities? Find out!
- Learn the "Pledge of Allegiance."

Massachusetts

- Around the time of the Revolutionary War, whaling was an important part of Massachusetts' economy. Whaling ships went out to sea for months at a time to hunt for whales. The most valuable part of the whale was the oil stored in the whale's blubber. In the days before electricity, whale oil was burned in lamps to light homes. If you had been a student in Massachusetts at that time, you might have studied by the light of a whale-oil lamp. Check out a book from the library to find more about the whaling industry.
- Go to your local library and find a book of Phillis Wheatley's poetry.

Maine

- Make a dish combining seafood and blueberries!
- Take a mile-long hike. How many minutes did your hike take? Multiply to find out how long it would take for you to walk the entire Appalachian Trail.
- Can you learn a few words in the Abenaki language? http://westernabenaki.com/

New Hampshire

- Read "The Road Not Taken" by Robert Frost. Make a drawing of the poem's New England images.
- New Hampshirite Sarah Hale convinced President Lincoln to make Thanksgiving a national holiday. Make a Thanksgiving meal any day of the week. Make it a simple meal of Thanksgiving, like the first Pilgrims might have eaten. It is good to remember that the celebration is about giving thanks—not about buying expensive food and eating until we burst.

A Nation of Immigrants

Please open your text to page 21. Find the "Mysteries of History." Now carefully re-read the two paragraphs that begin *"Explorers from other lands..."* and *"In time, immigrants came to America..."* How many of the countries listed in these paragraphs can you find on a map? Use a map or globe to find the countries.

Write the names of the countries on the lines. Then draw a line from the name of the country to its location on the map. The first one is done for you.

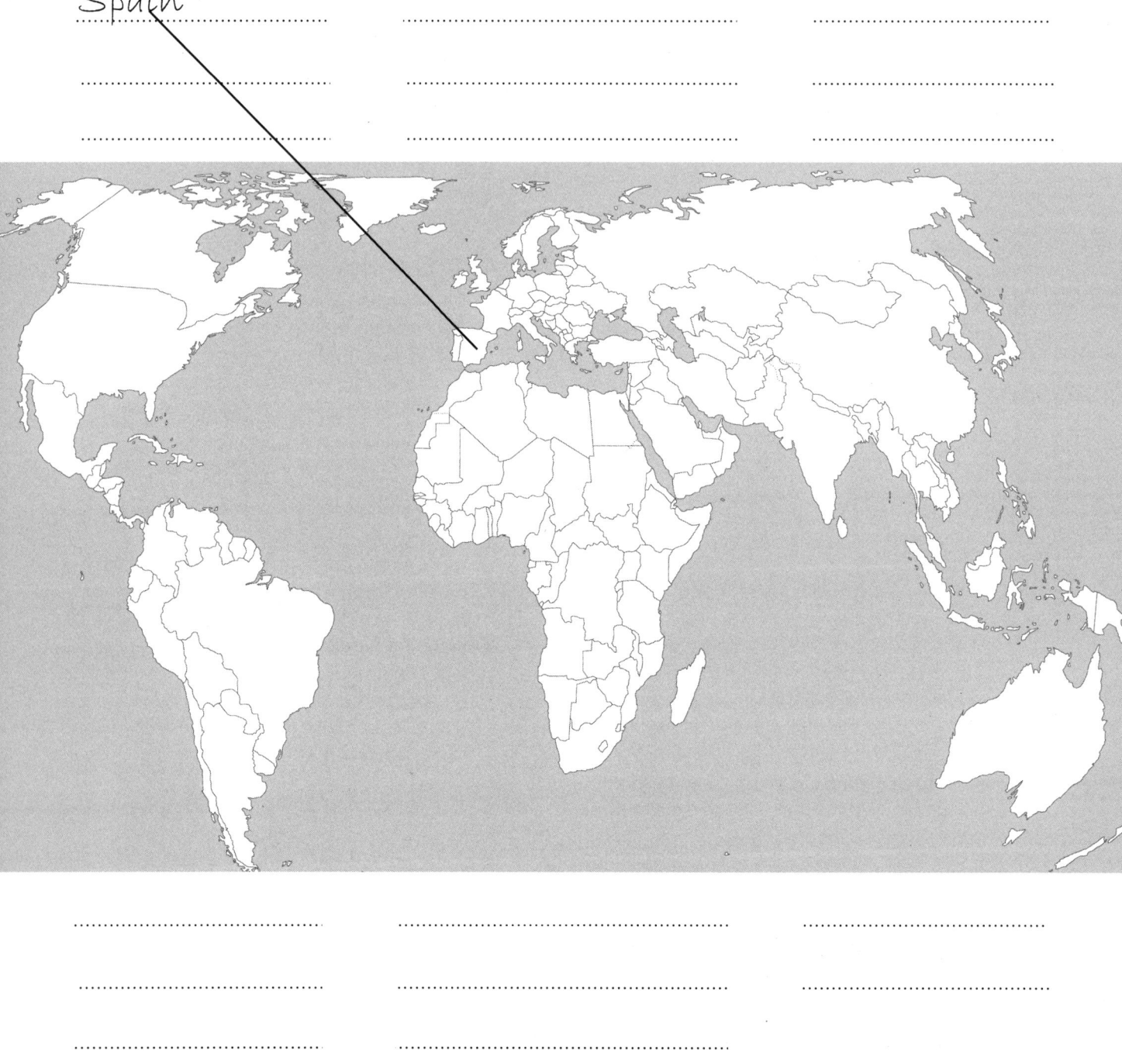

Spain

Northeastern Region—New England

Maps and Caps

The New England states are: **Connecticut, Maine, Massachusetts, New Hampshire, Rhode Island,** and **Vermont.**

Write the names on the correct states. Research and find the capitals of the states and write their names in as well.

Now make a hand-drawn copy of this map. In pencil, write in tiny, tiny letters the state and capital names on your hand-drawn map, too.

Please save these maps, because you will use them again. How quickly can you memorize the states and their capitals?

Northeastern Region—New England

Matching Clue Words: Connecticut

Directions: Read about Connecticut in your text. Use clue words to help find the answers as you read. Use words from the box to fill in the blanks for questions 1-6. (The answers to questions 7 and 8 are found in the textbook only.)

| Benedict Arnold | The Great Compromise | factories |
| Fr. Michael J. McGivney | The Fundamental Orders | Nathan Hale |

1. Connecticut was the first colony to have a set of rules that were a type of constitution. These rules were called ....

2. This patriot was willing to fight and die for his country.
   ....

3. This famous American Revolutionary War general betrayed his country and joined the British side, a traitor fighting against his friends.
   ....

4. When the U.S. Constitution—the laws that rule our country—was being written, delegates argued about the best way for states to be represented fairly. They decided to have a Senate and a House of Representatives to be fair to big states and small. This idea was called
   ....

5. An industrial state is one in which people make their living working in
   ....

Northeastern Region—New England

6. This kind priest started the Knights of Columbus.

   ....

7. Connecticut is best known for its production of what type of equipment? Name two kinds of equipment manufactured here.

   ....

   ....

8. What phrase were the Knights partly responsible for having added to the Pledge of Allegiance?

   ....

The "Five W" Clue Words, Part I

You have learned to find **bolded** and *italicized* clue words to open the door to understanding what you read. But oftentimes, clue words are not in bold or italics. We can still find these clue words if we look for these five things:

Who   What   When   Where   Why

Notice that sometimes the answer is one or two words, but at other times the answer is several words in a group. The answers are in bold this time, but when you read, ask yourself:

Who is this about? See how the bolded words tell who? Circle the words that tell who.

> Last Saturday, **Jumpy Jerome** bounced wildly around the house because he had no indoor manners at all.

For now, think of *What* as asking *what* is this about, or *(did)What*?

The bolded words tell "(did)What" or what happened. Circle the "(did)what" words.

> Last Saturday, Jumpy Jerome **bounced wildly** around the house because he had no indoor manners at all.

When did it happen? The bolded words tell when. Circle the words that tell when.

> **Last Saturday,** Jumpy Jerome bounced wildly around the house because he had no indoor manners at all.

Where did it happen, or where is it? Circle the words that tell where.

> Last Saturday, Jumpy Jerome bounced wildly **around the house** because he had no indoor manners at all.

Why did it happen? The bolded words tell why. Circle the words that tell why.

> Last Saturday, Jumpy Jerome bounced wildly around the house **because he had no indoor manners at all.**

It's easy to be a detective and find information when you look for the "5 W" clue words!

The "Five W" Clue Words, Part II

Now you are ready to try this clue-word trick yourself. Read the sentences below. Look for the "5 W's." Circle the answers. (Sometimes the answer will be a group of several words in the sentence.)

Who   (did)What   When   Where   Why

1. *Who* is this about? Circle the part of the sentence that tells who.

    The French and British both wanted the same land.

2. *What* is this about? Circle the part of the sentence that tells what they did ([did]What).

    The French and British started to fight over the lands they had explored.

3. *When* did it happen? Circle the part of the sentence that tells when it happened.

    In the 1750s, some Native American tribes joined the French side.

4. *Where* did it happen, or where is it? Circle the part that tells where.

    The lands that the French and British fought over were mostly in northeastern America.

5. *Why* did it happen? Circle the sentence that tells why the French and British battled.

    European countries explored America. Both the French and the British wanted the same land. In the 1750s, Native Americans joined the French to fight against the British. Within a few years, the British defeated, or beat, the French. Now the British owned most of the land that France had claimed.

6. Using all these clues, on a separate piece of paper, write a sentence or two about the French and Indian War that tells Who, (did)What, and When.

Learning the States:
Can you identify the states and their capitals yet? Cover the tiny, tiny state and capital labels on your hand-drawn map with a game piece, or torn piece of paper. Can you correctly identify states and capitals? (Give your workbook to someone who can check your answers as you say the names aloud.)

Northeastern Region—New England

"Dig Up" the Correct Word: Maine

Directions: Read about Maine. Print the correct words from the box on the blank lines. Use the tricks for finding clue words to help find the answers as you read.

Portland Head Light lighthouse	John Cabot	Massachusetts Bay Colony
Native Americans	Vikings	respect
Fr. Sebastien Rale	Appalachians	ships

1. Who may have sailed across the Atlantic to Maine in the year 1000?
   ....

2. Which English explorer is given credit for discovering Maine?
   ....

3. In 1677, the English settlements were made part of the ....

4. Who lost most of their land in unfair treaties? ....

5. To help ships safely travel Maine's seacoast, what was built?
   ....

6. Which mountains cross the state of Maine? ....

7. Long ago, Maine's most important industry was the building of what?
   ....

8. Name the French priest who brought the Catholic Faith to the Abenaki tribe.
   ....

9. Father Rale believed Abenakis should be treated with the same ....
   that one would give Europeans.

Northeastern Region—New England

Massachusetts: Pilgrims and Puritans

Read the sentences below. Look for the "5 W's." Circle the answers.

      Who   **(did)What**   **When**   **Where**   **Why**

1. *Who* is this about? Circle the part of the sentence that tells who.

    In 1620, Pilgrims landed not far from a spot they named Plymouth.

2. *What* is this about? Circle the part of the sentence that tells what they did.

    In 1620, Pilgrims started the settlement of Plymouth.

3. *When* did it happen? Circle the part of the sentence that tells when it happened.

    In 1620, Pilgrims started the settlement of Plymouth.

4. *Where* did it happen, or where is it? Circle the part that tells where.

    In 1620, Pilgrims started the settlement of Plymouth, Massachusetts.

5. *Why* did it happen? Circle the sentence that tells why the Pilgrims had a difficult time.

    At first, the Pilgrims had a hard time in this new land. Most of them weren't farmers, and the land and plants were very different from what they were used to in England. But kind Native Americans taught the Pilgrims how to grow crops and how to hunt animals in the forests.

Social Studies: Then and Now

Pilgrim and Native American societies were at first very different. But each culture learned from the other. What did the Pilgrims learn from the Native Americans? How do you think history might have been different if the Pilgrims hadn't wanted to learn a new way? Do you think there would be a Plymouth, Massachusetts today? Do you see how history—what happened then—affects how we live now?

Learning the States:
Can you identify the states and their capitals yet? Time to practice! Give someone your map and have them test you. How did you do?

Northeastern Region—New England

"Dig Up" the Correct Words: Massachusetts

Directions: Read about Massachusetts. Print the correct words from the box on the blank lines. Use the tricks for finding clue words to help find the answers as you read.

Boston Massacre	Paul Revere	Massasoit
Squanto	Samoset	Massachusetts Bay Colony
Boston Tea Party	Phillis Wheatley	Plymouth

1. Which settlement did the Pilgrims start? ....

2. Which colony did the Puritans start? ....

3. What were the names of the Native Americans who helped the Pilgrims?
   ....

4. More than 100 years after the Pilgrims, unfair British laws angered the Americans, who gathered in a crowd to protest. British troops fired into the Americans, killing five. This was the ....

5. Later, patriots in disguise protested against British taxes on tea by dumping tea into Boston Harbor. This event was known as the ....

6. This brave citizen galloped his horse through town, warning people that British troops were coming to attack.
   ....

7. This young slave was educated and set free by her owners. She became a great poet.
   ....

8. On a separate piece of paper, and in your own words, tell some of the things that made Abigail Adams a great patriot and "Founding Mother."

More about Massachusetts

1. You remember that ***natural resources*** are useful things that are found in the water or in the soil, like lobsters, trees, or gold. An ***economy*** is the making, buying, and selling of goods that creates jobs. Name the natural resource that is important to the economy of Massachusetts.
   ....

2. The ***American Industrial Revolution*** began in Massachusetts, and it's still a major manufacturing state. Name two things that are manufactured in factories here today.
   ....

3. Before the Industrial Revolution, there were no big machines. People mostly made things
   a. at the store b. at home c. in a factory

4. Industry, or factory work, changed the economy and the way people worked. In factories, products could be made
   a. newer b. more quickly and cheaply c. by silversmiths

5. The Puritans came to Massachusetts for religious freedom, but anyone who did not follow the Puritan faith was treated unfairly, or
   a. persecuted b. population c. Pilgrim

6. America's first bishop was
   a. John Adams b. John Carroll c. Charles Bullfinch

7. A political party that hated immigrants and Catholics, and set fire to Catholic churches and schools, was called the
   a. Know-It-Alls b. Nonsense c. Know-Nothings

Social Studies: Then and Now
Before the Industrial Revolution, most people worked on farms or made things in their own homes. On a separate piece of paper, tell where your family members and neighbors work now. Could they do their jobs at home? What would our lives be like now if the Industrial Revolution had never happened? Do you see how history—what happened then—affects how we now live? Do you see that the way we live now also will, in time, be part of history?

Northeastern Region—New England

Other New England States and the Bill of Rights

1. Look at a map of the entire United States, showing the Pacific and Atlantic Oceans. Find New Hampshire and Vermont. Then answer the question. Did you notice that the economies of most New England states include the fishing industry? Why do you think that the fishing industry is not a big part of New Hampshire and Vermont's economies?

   ....

   ....

   ....

2. Freedom of speech and freedom of religion are only two of ten rights listed in the

    a. Civil Rights   b. Bill of Rights   c. right to assemble

3. Who was kicked out of the Massachusetts Bay Colony because he spoke in favor of religious freedom?

    a. Roger Williams   b. William Carroll   c. Jolly Roger

4. Who started the colony of Rhode Island?

    a. William Carroll   b. Roger Williams   c. Ethan Allen

5. Vermont was discovered by French explorer Samuel de Champlain, but the British took the land away from France during the

    a. Revolutionary War   b. French and Indian War

6. An army of "patriot farmers" from Vermont, the "Green Mountain Boys," captured which British fort?

    a. Fort Ticonderoga   b. Fort Vermont   c. Fort Arnold

7. Who gathered these farmers together to create his own "army"?

    a. General Washington   b. Colonel Benedict Arnold   c. Ethan Allen

Time to Grab Maps and Thinking Caps!

Map Challenge

Carefully study the map for this region on page 9. Do you have the states and capitals memorized? Good! Get a fresh piece of paper, turn the map over, and draw from memory the map with all the states in the region. Label the state names and capitals. When you are done, compare the two maps. How did you do? (You will soon be tested on the states and their capitals.) If your map isn't quite right, re-draw it now.

Mapping the Economy

Connecticut, Maine, Massachusetts, New Hampshire, Rhode Island, Vermont

Grab your hand-drawn map, and put on your thinking cap! Turn to pages 18-20 in your textbook. What types of factory goods are produced in Connecticut? Find at least two products that are manufactured here. Draw small symbols or simple pictures of these products on your map, on the state of Connecticut.

Read a bit farther to find out what else people of the state produce for the state's economy. Pick two more products and draw those on your map as well.

There is one natural resource—something found naturally in the waters, or in or on the soil—that is mentioned in the text. Can you find it? I'll give you a clue: this product is something that is found naturally in the water, caught, and then sold in markets and restaurants. Draw a symbol of this natural resource in the ocean next to Connecticut.

Do this same exercise for the rest of the states studied in the New England region. Look for things that make up an economy by providing jobs, and things that people buy and sell. Be sure to include natural resources! Pick two things that are manufactured, and two natural resources to draw for each state. (If the textbook lists only one item for a state, you may draw just one item.)

Northeastern Region—New England

Thinking Caps

When you have finished your map, put on your thinking cap! In your textbook, turn back to the page titled "New England Region," page 17. See what you can find out about the climate, weather, and geography, or the type of land found in this region. Is the region mostly hot, bare deserts, or does it have mountains covered with trees? Is it near the ocean, or miles and miles away from any water?

On a separate piece of paper, write the name of the region. Then write the words that you have found that tell about climate, weather, and geography. Your paper should look something like this:

#1. The New England Region
rainy, cloudy spring
hot summer
snowy winter
mountains

On the same piece of paper, do the same with the state of Connecticut. Write any words that you have found that tell about climate, weather, and geography.

#2. Connecticut
eastern seaboard (This means it's next to the sea.)
Connecticut River
Thimble Islands
water access
beaches

Now, adjust your thinking cap and put it to use. In your map assignment, you discovered and drew symbols of jobs and industry that make up this region's economy. With this information about the economy, climate, and geography, why do you think that Connecticut has the jobs that it does? Did the people who live in the state make good use of the land, water, and natural resources that God had provided? They must have used their thinking caps, too!

Now, we will write a sentence or two that tell why the jobs and climate, geography, and natural resources fit so well together:

> #3. Why
> Because this state is close to the ocean, fishermen can catch lobster and submarines can be launched into the Atlantic Ocean. If submarines are manufactured here, it makes sense that other military equipment like helicopters could be made here, too.

See how easy that was? Now do the same thing for the rest of the states in the New England Region, including New Hampshire, Rhode Island, and Vermont. Remember to include parts #1, #2, and #3.

Northeastern Region — New England

Northeastern Region: New England Review/Test

(Review/Test pages may be used as review, for testing, or both.)

1. Weather in the New England region is

    a. warm all year 'round
    b. warm in the summer with snowy winters

2. Useful things, like fish or trees, that are found in the water or in or on the soil are called

    a. natural wonders
    b. natural resources
    c. economy

3. Before the Industrial Revolution, most people worked

    a. at home
    b. in factories
    c. on the sea

4. The making, selling, and buying of goods that creates jobs is called

    a. making things
    b. natural resources
    c. an economy

5. The French and Indian war was fought because the French and British wanted

    a. freedom of speech
    b. the same land
    c. a Tea Party

6. People who come from far away to settle in a new land are called

    a. immigrants
    b. patriots
    c. strangers

7. Early American settlements were started by people from other countries who wanted the land for their own countries. These settlements that belonged to another country were called

    a. states
    b. countries
    c. colonies

8. The first Thanksgiving was celebrated by the

    a. Pilgrims and Indians
    b. French and Indians
    c. French and British

9. A person who loves his country so much that he is willing to die for it is called a
   a. silversmith   b. patriot   c. senator

10. By the time the Revolutionary War started, all thirteen colonies were owned by
    a. the Dutch   b. the French   c. the British

11. The Revolutionary War was fought because the British forced Americans to follow
    a. the leader   b. unfair rules or laws   c. a Constitution

12. The set of laws that now rule our country is called
    a. the Constitution   b. The Great Compromise   c. the Declaration of Independence

13. A system of leaders, laws, and rules by which a nation lives is called a
    a. government   b. president   c. colony

14. Our freedom of religion and freedom of speech are two of ten freedoms listed in the
    a. government   b. Independence Day   c. Bill of Rights

15. Another word for farming is
    a. agriculture   b. industry   c. natural resource

Draw lines to match the states with their capitals:

16. New Hampshire   Augusta

17. Rhode Island   Boston

18. Vermont   Concord

19. Connecticut   Montpelier

20. Maine   Hartford

21. Massachusetts   Providence

Review/Test

22-28. Draw lines to match the state names with their locations.

New Hampshire

Rhode Island

Vermont

Connecticut

Maine

Massachusetts

Northeastern Region
MID-ATLANTIC

Lessons Alive!

Teacher's Note: *For age-appropriate research, the library is sometimes preferable to the internet. When the historical figure or event plays a significant but potentially controversial role in history, library books are suggested instead of online research. (E.g., Benjamin Franklin, below.)*

New York

Immigration and Culture

- Make a collage of Americans from many countries and cultures who immigrated to and live in New York. Title your collage, "What is an American?" Cut pictures from magazines or draw pictures. If you cannot use magazines, with your teacher's permission, you might find photos online.

- "Visit" New York City at home. With your parent, "tour" the Metropolitan Museum of Art at *https://www.metmuseum.org/art/online-features/met-360-project*. (Parent should preview videos and images first for age-appropriate content.) Make an art gallery of your original work. Put on a play. Create your own "Coney Island" hotdog stand and serve lunch!

- Remember that you don't have to live in New York to discover culture. Each community has its own unique culture. Visit a local history or art museum or community theater. No skyscrapers? Find the tallest building in your town.

- Find out more about the North American Martyrs and St. Isaac Jogues and Companions.

Pennsylvania

Immigration, Culture, and American Saints

- Read and discuss the Declaration of Independence and also the famous Preamble of the Constitution; both were signed in Pennsylvania.

- Pick either the first two sentences of the Declaration or the Preamble for this activity. Either by hand or on the computer, print the words on large cards and cut them into pieces. Put the words back together while discussing the meaning of the words. Time yourself and see if you can beat your record each time. You'll be surprised at how quickly you can memorize the first lines of these most important documents.

- Just this once, plan a lunch or dinner consisting of Pennsylvania snack food. Perhaps include hoagies, or Philly cheese steak. Pittsburgh's Primanti Brothers invented a famous sandwich just for factory workers so they could eat an entire meal with one hand, so the workers could keep working as they ate. Potato chips or French fries are placed *inside* the sandwiches, which are served wrapped in waxed paper instead of on plates.

- St. Katharine Drexel gave away her entire fortune of $22 million dollars, keeping none for herself. (What an example of generosity and unselfishness this saint set for us!) Keeping in mind the Corporal Works of Mercy, make a list of whom you could help and how you could change the world for the better if you could give away the same amount of money. The only rule in this activity is that you can't spend more than $2 million in one place.

- Find out more about the remarkable statesman and patriot, Benjamin Franklin. Check out a library book that tells about his life, experiments, and inventions.

- Challenge: Can you memorize the Gettysburg Address?

New Jersey

Revolutionary War, Immigration, and Culture

- Memorize Emma Lazarus' poem found on the Statue of Liberty (found in your text with New York, as the statue is near both New York and New Jersey).

- What else can you discover about Emma Lazarus; the Statue of Liberty; and Ellis Island, through which so many immigrants first entered America and set foot on American soil?

- Were your ancestors immigrants? How did our country's history of immigration change the way your family lives today? How might your life have been different if your ancestors had never come to this land? Write a story about what your life might be like now if your ancestors had never come to America.

- Find out more about General George Washington, Valley Forge, and Baron von Steuben. Or find out more about the Hessians and the Revolutionary War battle at Trenton, New Jersey.

- In New Jersey, Campbell launched an industry with its canned soups. Invent a new soup from scratch. Write to Campbell's and suggest your new flavor! (Remember that all inventions, even Campbell's soups, began because someone like you put on his thinking cap, rolled up their sleeves, and set to work.)

- With your teacher's help, make that New Jersey treat: saltwater taffy.

Maps and Caps

The Mid-Atlantic states are: **New York, New Jersey,** and **Pennsylvania.**

Write the names on the correct states. Research and find the capitals of the states and write their names in as well.

Now make a hand-drawn copy of this map. In pencil, write in tiny, tiny letters the state and capital names on your hand-drawn map, too.

Please save these maps, because you will use them again. How quickly can you memorize the states and their capitals?

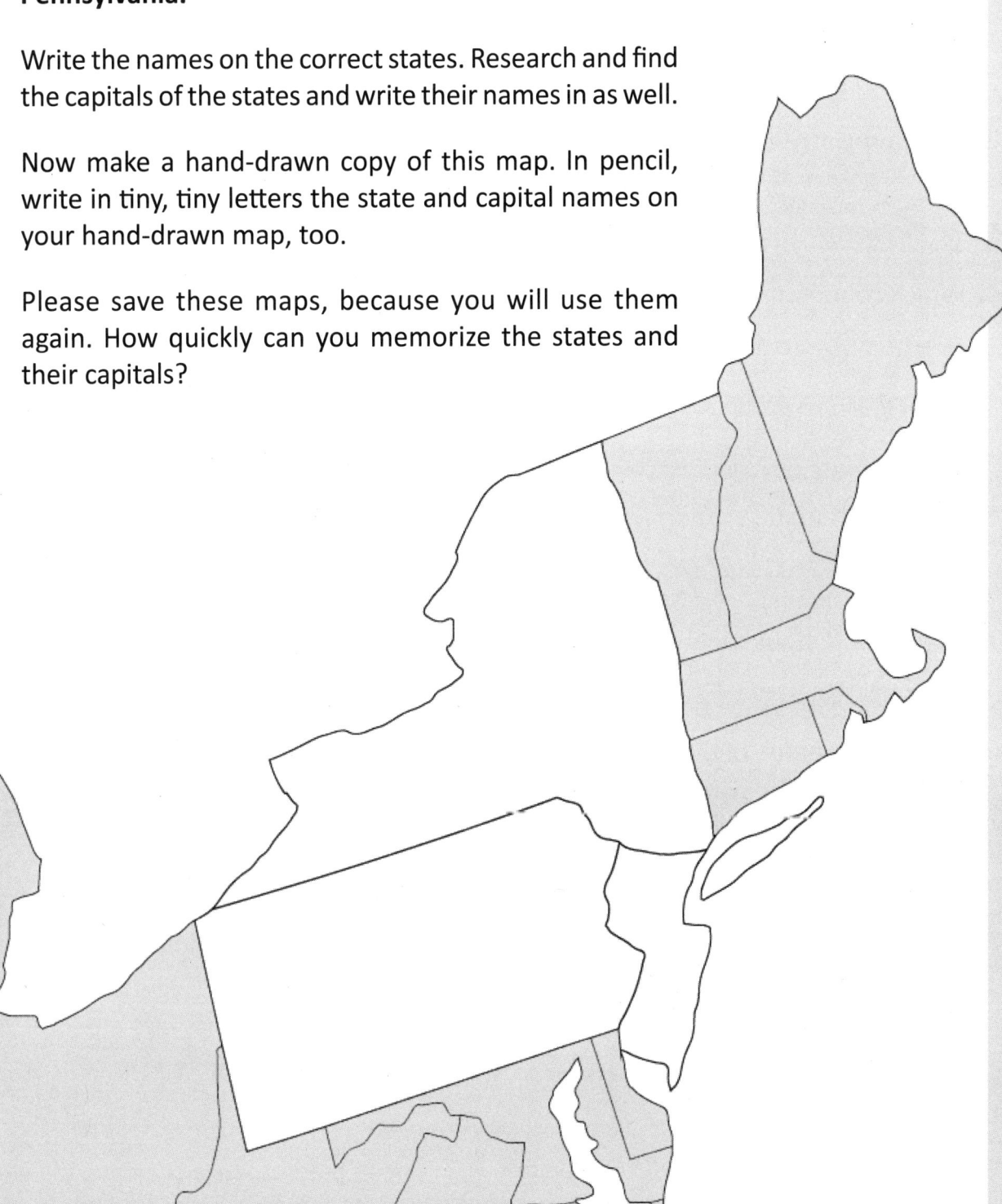

Northeastern Region—Mid-Atlantic

27

The Mid-Atlantic Region

Who   (did)What   When   Where   Why

1. Which countries originally explored and settled this region?
   ....

2. When was the Mid-Atlantic region explored? ....

3. Which country eventually took complete control of the region?
   ....

New York

4. Which country first colonized the state we now call New York? ....
   ....

5. What was the name first given by the Dutch to their colony?
   ....

6. Large, man-made waterways, dug to make trade and travel easier, were called
   ....

7. The most famous canal that joined Lake Erie with rivers and lakes in New York was called ....

8. What is the name of the famous statue that immigrants saw as they sailed into New York harbor? Also name the New York island on which many immigrants first set foot on American soil.
   ....

9. Name four saints who lived or ministered in this Mid-Atlantic region.
   ....
   ....

Learning the States:

Can you identify the states and their capitals yet? Time to practice! Give someone the map in your workbook and ask them to test you. Cover the state and capital labels on your hand-drawn map and identify each state and capital. How did you do?

New Jersey and Pennsylvania

10. The colony of Pennsylvania was named after this man, who allowed people of any religion to settle in "his" colony.

   ....

11. Flat lands are called this:

    a. mountains   b. valleys   c. plains

12. Pennsylvania's southern border is also a kind of boundary line that "separates" North from South. This border or line is called the

    a. Mason-Dixon Line   b. William Penn Line   c. Keystone Line

13. Arguments between northern and southern states eventually exploded into the

    a. French and Indian War   b. Revolutionary War   c. Civil War

14. At the time of the Civil War, the president of the United States was

    a. George Washington   b. Abraham Lincoln   c. William Penn

15. This amazing Revolutionary War patriot was one of the Founding Fathers of our nation. He was an inventor who experimented with electricity; an author; musician; and much more.

    a. George Washington   b. John Carroll   c. Benjamin Franklin

16. Which Pennsylvania saints, a bishop and a religious sister, ministered especially to African-Americans and Native Americans?

   ....

17. New Jersey's Menlo Park was the workplace of this famous inventor of many electrical items that improved life for people around the world.

   ....

Social Studies: Then and Now
While great thinkers and inventors Benjamin Franklin and Thomas Edison did not "invent" electricity, their experiments and inventions helped bring us into the "electric age." Go through your home and try to make a list of everything that uses electricity. How might your life—and history— be different if great thinkers and inventors like Benjamin Franklin and Thomas Edison had never been born, or hadn't used the skills that God gave them?

Northeastern Region—Mid-Atlantic

Time to Grab Maps and Thinking Caps!

Map Challenge

Carefully study the map for this region on page 27. Do you have the states and capitals memorized? Good! Get a fresh piece of paper, turn the map over, and draw from memory the map with all the states in the region. Label the state names and capitals. When you are done, compare the two maps. How did you do? (You will soon be tested on the states and their capitals.) If your map isn't quite right, re-draw it now.

Mapping the Economy

New York, New Jersey, Pennsylvania

Grab your hand-drawn map, and put on your thinking cap! Now, turn to these states in your textbook. What types of factory goods are produced in these states? Starting with the first state, find at least two products that are manufactured for each state. Draw small symbols or pictures of these products on your map, on the states where they are manufactured.

What else do the people of these states produce for the state's economy? Pick two more products for each state and draw those on your map as well. Look for things that make up an economy by providing jobs, and things that people buy and sell. Be sure to include natural resources!

Midwestern Region
EAST NORTH-CENTRAL

Lessons Alive!

Ohio

Faith, Perseverance, and Hard Work Benefit Society

- How did escaping slaves find their way to freedom in the North? In constant danger of discovery, and traveling mostly at night, how could they find their way through dark woods and unfamiliar territory? (Their faith in God and bravery set an example for us!) Find out about the North Star, the Big Dipper constellation, and the song, "Follow the Drinking Gourd." Can you find this constellation in the night sky? Can you locate the North Star?

- Thomas Edison experimented and invented things even as a child. While his experiments often failed, he didn't stop trying. He often began his experiments with things that he had on hand. What can you invent? (Earmuffs were invented by a teenager using his imagination, a piece of wire, and tufts of fur.) See what you can invent from nothing more than what's lying around the house. No buying anything!

Michigan

Culture, Economy

- When cars were first produced, most people couldn't imagine that they would be much more than a passing "fad." Many roads weren't much more than dirt trails, and didn't go all the way across country as they do today. People traveled by train, or horse and buggy. Check out "Horatio's Drive: America's First Road Trip," produced by PBS and Ken Burns, which tells the fascinating and sometimes funny story of the first cross-country trip by automobile in 1903.

- Can you say "mnemonic device" quickly three times? A mnemonic device, or trick to memorize things, is a useful tool to help us study. A mnemonic device that will help you to learn the names of the Great Lakes is to remember "HOMES." (HOMES is an acronym made up of the first letter in the name of each lake.) How quickly can you memorize the names of the lakes? Time yourself, and then share the trick with your family.

    Huron
    Ontario
    Michigan
    Erie
    Superior

Illinois

Perseverance, Hard Work, and Honesty Benefit Society

- President Abraham Lincoln made a name for himself in Illinois, which is known as the "Land of Lincoln." Find out about this man who was born into poverty, who through hard work and study taught himself to be a lawyer—and was later elected President.

- Find out more about the Great Chicago Fire. Do you think the reporter who wrote a story about the fire being started by Mrs. O'Leary's cow was reporting truthfully? Why is it important to tell the truth always, including at the places where we work? How can we make wise decisions about what happens in our society if news reporters in the *media* (newspaper, radio, TV, and internet news) don't report truthfully? After reading more about the Great Chicago Fire, pretend that you are a TV reporter and write a short news article telling what really happened in the great fire. Then present your report at dinnertime as the "nightly news."

Indiana

Culture

- Celebrate a gift that came to us from Native American tribes. Make some popcorn!

Wisconsin

Faith, Immigration, and Culture

- Wisconsin has a rich history of immigration. With towns named Krakow, Pulaski, Sobieski, and Poland, can you "detect" where many of these immigrants came from? *First Farm in the Valley: Anna's Story* tells the story of one Polish Catholic immigrant family, and their Polish Catholic culture and traditions. Perhaps you would like to sing the Angelus before your noon meal as they did, or add Polish Name Day or Easter traditions mentioned in this book to your family traditions.

- "E Pluribus Unum": this Latin phrase means "out of many, one." This phrase appears on our coins, and also on the Seal of the United States. It refers to the great blessing of those who immigrated from many countries, sharing their gifts and culture, to become one people: Americans. Find out on which of your coins this phrase appears.

- Wisconsin's dairy industry produces not only milk and butter, but also the state's famous cheeses. Pick out four or five different cheeses that you have never before tasted. Plan a lunch or snack around these cheese products. Perhaps you'll have cheese and crackers, cheese melts, salad with cheese cubes, or maybe you'll invent a new cheese pizza!

Maps and Caps

The East North-Central states are: **Illinois, Indiana, Michigan, Ohio, Wisconsin.** Write the names on the correct states. Research and find the capitals of the states and write their names in as well.

Now make a hand-drawn copy of this map. In pencil, write in tiny, tiny letters the state and capital names on your hand-drawn map, too.

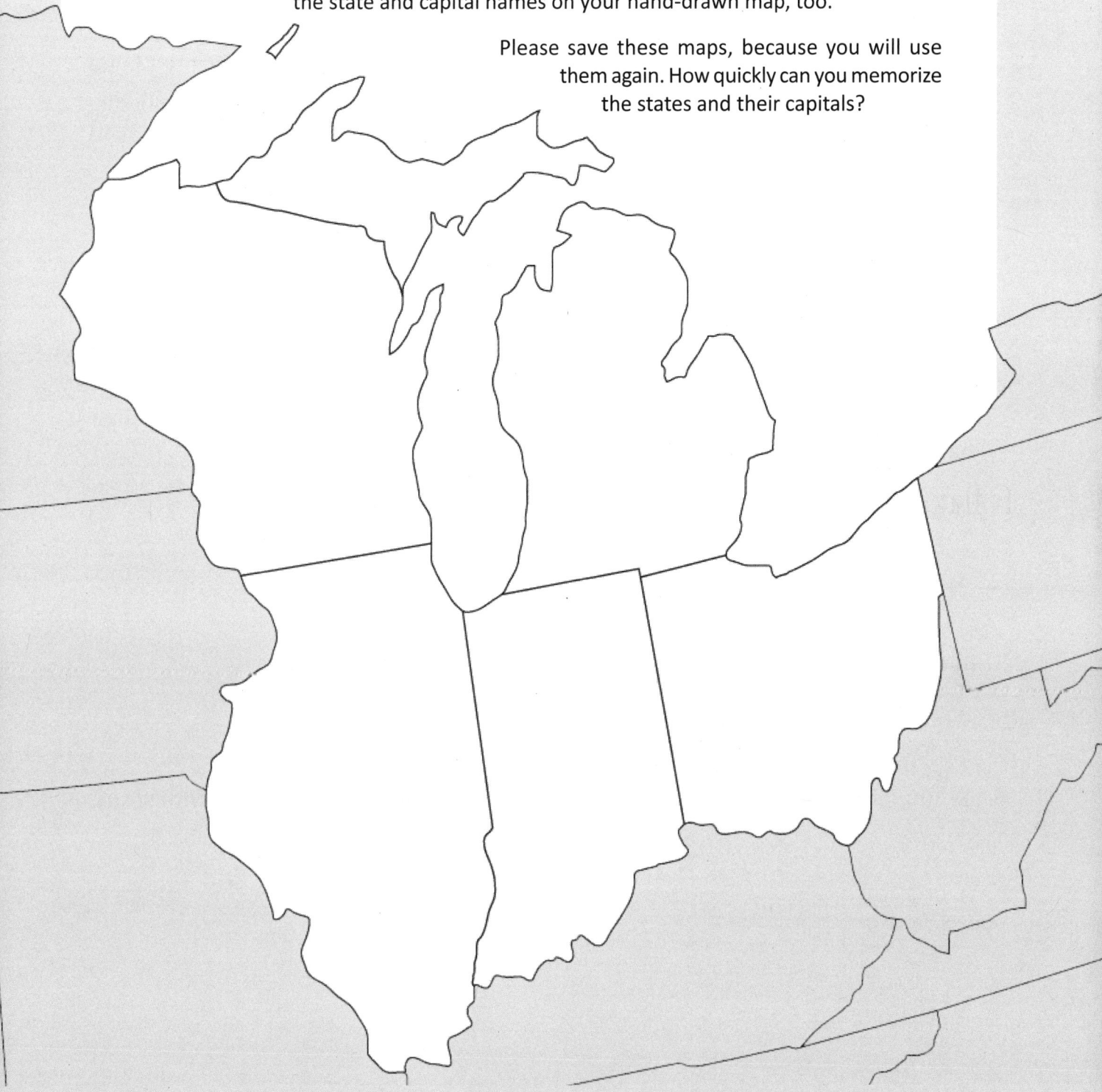

Please save these maps, because you will use them again. How quickly can you memorize the states and their capitals?

Midwestern Region—East North-Central

What Have You Learned?
Midwestern Region: East North-Central

Map Study:

1. Look at a map of the United States. The original 13 colonies stretched from Maine in the north to Georgia in the south. Find these states, then find Illinois, Indiana, Michigan, Ohio, and Wisconsin. Why do you think this new region was first called the "Northwest Territory"?

   ....

   ....

   ....

2. The East North-Central states are called the "Great Lakes States" because each state is joined to one of these lakes. Find the five Great Lakes on a U.S. map; write their names here:

   ....

   ....

   ....

3. Indiana was named for the people who first lived there; they were

   ....

4. When faced with hardship, Mother Theodore often told her sisters, "With Jesus,

   ....

   .... "

5. Native American tribes trapped animals and took their furs to French traders. The French traded items that were useful to the tribes, like knives and axes, for the furs which would be made into clothing and hats. This "buying and selling" of furs was called the

   a. fur trade   b. fur buying   c. knife and axe trade

6. A piece of land surrounded by water on three sides, but still connected to the mainland is:

   a. an island   b. a river   c. a peninsula

7. This priest founded the first European settlement in Michigan.

   a. Fr. Donald Pelotte   b. Fr. Jacques Marquette   c. Fr. John Neumann

8. This man joined the priest named above in exploring up and down the Mississippi River.

   a. Nathan Hale   b. Fr. Isaac Jogues   c. Louis Joliet

Family Names from History
"Mystery of History"

For fun and extra credit:

You have read about the different ways that people were given family names. Some names like Crown (*Corona* in Spanish) indicate that people worked for the King. Others, like Church (*Iglesia* in Spanish) indicate that people worked for, or lived near, a church. Some names, like Baker, are easy to figure out. But others take a little more detective work.

Directions:

The following family names tell which job the person may have had, or who they worked for. Look the names up in the dictionary. Then write the type of job the person did on the line.

1. Miller ....
2. Archer ....
3. Fletcher ....
4. Piper ....
5. Cooper ....
6. Smith ....
7. Glazier ....
8. Brewer ....
9. Weaver ....

For extra credit, look through a telephone book and see how many other family names you can spot that were types of jobs. Earn one extra point for each name.

....

....

Time to Grab Maps and Thinking Caps!

Map Challenge

Carefully study the map for this region on page 33. Do you have the states and capitals memorized? Good! Get a fresh piece of paper, turn the map over, and draw from memory the map with all the states in this region. Label the state names and capitals. When you are done, compare the two maps. How did you do? (You will soon be tested on the states and their capitals.) If your map isn't quite right, re-draw it now.

Mapping the Economy

Illinois, Indiana, Michigan, Ohio, Wisconsin

Grab your hand-drawn map, and put on your thinking cap! Now, turn to these states in your textbook. What types of factory goods are produced in these states? Starting with the first state, find at least two products that are manufactured for each state. Draw small symbols or pictures of these products on your map, on the states where they are manufactured.

What else do the people of these states produce for the state's economy? Pick two more products for each state and draw those on your map as well. Look for things that make up an economy by providing jobs, and things that people buy and sell. Be sure to include natural resources!

Put on Those Thinking Caps

Turn back to the page titled "East North-Central Region" in your textbook, page 63. Read this page to find out about the climate, weather, and geography, or the type of land found in this region. Is the region mostly hot, bare deserts, or does it have mountains covered with trees? Is it near the ocean, or miles and miles away from any water?

On a separate piece of paper, write the name of the region. Then write the words that you have found that tell about climate, weather, and geography.

In your map assignment, you discovered and drew symbols of jobs and industries that make up this region's economy. With this information about the economy, climate, and geography, why do you think that this region has the jobs that it does? Do the people who live in the state make good use of the land, water, and natural resources that God has provided?

Now, write a sentence or two telling why the jobs and climate, geography, and natural resources fit so well together.

Midwestern Region—East North-Central

Northeastern and Midwestern Regions Review/Test

1. What was the name of the Dutch colony that later became New York?
   ....

2. Name the man-made waterway dug to join Lake Erie to rivers and lakes in New York.
   ....

3. Who was the first Native American to be declared a saint?
   ....

4. The Mason-Dixon Line separates the:

   a. men from the boys   b. East and West   c. North and South

5. The French priest .... , along with Louis Joliet, explored the lands up and down the .... River.

6. Who were the brothers that invented the airplane?
   ....

7-14. Draw lines to match the state names with their locations. Then write the correct capital on each state.

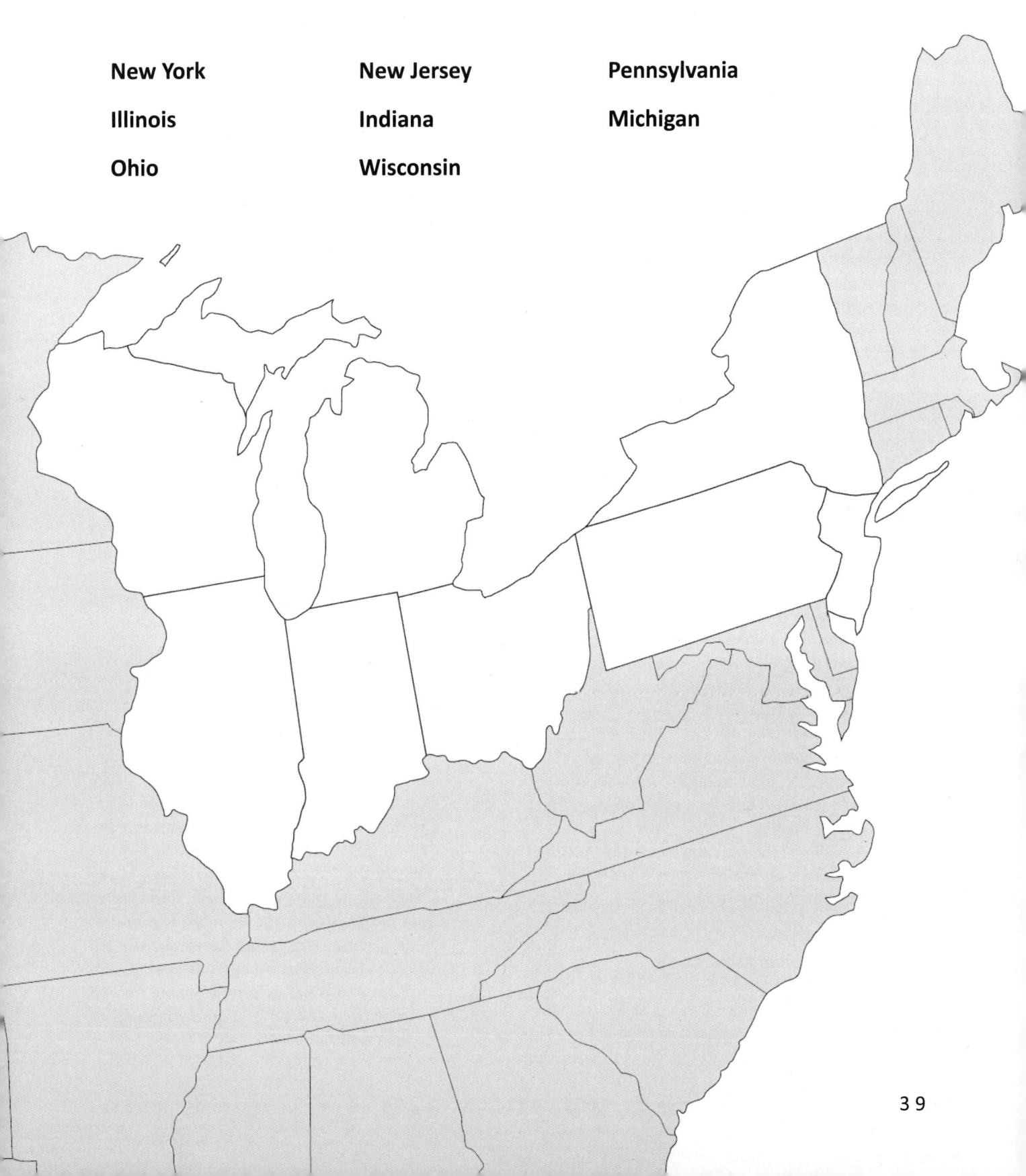

New York   **New Jersey**   **Pennsylvania**

Illinois   **Indiana**   **Michigan**

Ohio   **Wisconsin**

Midwestern Region
WEST NORTH-CENTRAL

Lessons Alive!

Kansas
A Culture of Thankful Determination
- Since Kansas' economy is centered mostly on agriculture, the Dust Bowl of the 1930s was devastating to the economy. Many lost their farms, homes, and jobs during this terrible time of drought. It was a time of great poverty, when families had to be extremely careful how they spent the little money they had. Mothers sewed clothing for their children from cloth flour sacks, and children kept the same pair of shoes until they wore holes through the soles. Then they cut cardboard insoles and wore them inside their shoes. Most lived by the saying, "Use it up; wear it out; make do, or do without." For the next month, every time you would like to buy something, think of a way that you can make something else serve the same purpose, or find a way to "make do" without the thing that you had wanted.
- If you had no food in the house but flour, milk, a little butter, and perhaps an egg, what kind of meals could you make? Ask your mother for ideas and see if you can make a "Dust Bowl" meal.
- Read about the Dust Bowl period in *The Green Coat: A Tale from the Dust Bowl Years*, and thank God for His many blessings.

Minnesota
A Culture of Thankful Perseverance
- Winter temperatures sometimes fall below -40°F in International Falls, where residents could complain about the weather, but instead find something fun to do in the weather that they have. (One popular sport played at their "Ice Box Festival" is "frozen turkey bowling.") Make up a fun activity that you can do when it seems too cold, too hot, or too rainy. Now think of another activity. Plan a festival that makes the most of the weather that you already have.

Nebraska
A Culture of Thankful Perseverance
- Pioneers to this prairie grassland had no trees or stone for building houses. They had to use what was available, which was sod. (Sod is simply square "bricks" of grass-covered dirt cut from the land.) Make an edible "sod" house. Bake a 9" x 13" pan of brownies, then cut the brownies into 1" x 2" rectangles and stack into walls. Use graham crackers for the roof.

South Dakota
Culture
- Our nation is made up of cultures within cultures. Even small towns may have their own cultural traditions. One South Dakota tradition is the yearly decorating of the Corn Palace, a building used for many events in the community of Mitchell. Each year, farmers supply the Palace with grains grown in the state. Straw, oats, milo, wheat, and corn of many colors are used to make the murals that decorate the Palace. Research the Corn Palace and be inspired by its designs. Create a "corn and grain" picture by gluing colored corn kernels and other natural materials to a square of cardboard.

Maps and Caps

The West North-Central states are: **Iowa, Kansas, Minnesota, Missouri, Nebraska, North Dakota, South Dakota.** Write the names on the correct states. Research and find the capitals of the states and write their names in as well.

Now make a hand-drawn copy of this map. In pencil, write in tiny, tiny letters the state and capital names on your hand-drawn map, too.

Please save these maps, because you will use them again. How quickly can you memorize the states and their capitals?

Midwestern Region—West North-Central

Midwestern Region: West North-Central

Draw lines from the definitions on the left to the words they define on the right.

1. an agreement written by Congress that said for every new slave state that came into the Union, a new free state had to come into the Union, too

2. the man who developed the steamboat

3. a "faster," Missouri-based mail delivery service

4. a girl whose bravery helped change laws on segregated schools

5. a saint called "The Woman Who Prays Always"

6. the huge stretch of flat prairie on which the West North-Central states sit

7. the Native American woman who led Lewis and Clark

8. a huge parcel of land which France sold to America, more than doubling the size of the United States

9. a machine that could send messages quickly over wires

10. With this Act, the American government promised free land to anyone who would live on it for five years.

11. a journey of discovery that explored the Louisiana Purchase and territory all the way to the Pacific Ocean

12. the man who invented the telegraph

13. a Nebraska priest who cared for troubled boys

14. an unfair system that separated and treated people differently because of the color of their skin

Louisiana Purchase

Pony Express

Great Plains

Samuel Morse

Robert Fulton

Missouri Compromise

telegraph

segregation

Lewis and Clark Expedition

Rose Philippine Duchesne

Homestead Act of 1862

Father Flanagan

Linda Brown

Sacagawea

Time to Grab Maps and Thinking Caps!

Map Challenge
Carefully study the map for this region on page 41. Do you have the states and capitals memorized? Good! Get a fresh piece of paper, turn the map over, and draw from memory the map with all the states in this region. Label the state names and capitals. When you are done, compare your map with the workbook map. How did you do? (You will soon be tested on the states and their capitals.) If your map isn't quite right, re-draw it now.

Mapping the Economy
Iowa, Kansas, Minnesota, Missouri, Nebraska, North Dakota, South Dakota

Grab your hand-drawn map, and put on your thinking cap! Now, turn to these states in your textbook. What types of factory goods are produced in these states? Starting with the first state, find at least two products that are manufactured for each state. Draw small symbols or pictures of these products on your map, on the states where they are manufactured.

What else do the people of these states produce for the state's economy? Pick two more products for each state and draw those on your map as well. Look for things that make up an economy by providing jobs, and things that people buy and sell. Be sure to include natural resources!

Put on Those Thinking Caps
Turn back to the page titled "West North-Central Region" in your textbook, page 83. Read this page to find out about the climate, weather, and geography, or the type of land found in this region. Is the region mostly hot, bare deserts, or does it have mountains covered with trees? Is it near the ocean, or miles and miles away from any water?

On a separate piece of paper, write the name of the region. Then write the words that you have found that tell about climate, weather, and geography.

In your map assignment, you discovered and drew symbols of jobs and industry that make up this region's economy. With this information about the economy, climate, and geography, why do you think that this region has the jobs that it does? Do the people who live in the state make good use of the land, water, and natural resources that God has provided?

Now, write a sentence or two telling why the jobs and climate, geography, and natural resources fit so well together.

Midwestern Region—West North-Central

Northeastern and Midwestern Regions Review/Test

1. What is the name of the famous statue that immigrants saw as they sailed into New York harbor?

    a. Statue of Ellis Island   b. Statue of Liberty

2. Pennsylvania's southern border is also a kind of boundary line that "separates" North from South. This border or line is called the

    a. Mason-Dixon Line   b. William Penn Line   c. Keystone Line

3. Name the five Great Lakes:

    ....

    ....

    ....

4. Louis Joliet joined this priest to explore up and down the Mississippi River.

    a. Fr. Jacques Marquette   b. Fr. Isaac Jogues   c. Fr. Flanagan

5. This agreement written by Congress said that for every new slave state that came into the Union, a new free state had to come into the Union, too.

    a. Mason-Dixon Line   b. Homestead Act   c. Missouri Compromise

6. What is the name of the huge parcel of land that France sold to the United States, which more than doubled the size of the United States?

    a. Homestead Act   b. Louisiana Purchase   c. Midwestern Purchase

7. The first Native-American to be declared a saint:

   a. Kateri Tekakwitha   b. Rose Philippine Duchesne   c. Robert Fulton

8. The girl whose bravery helped change unfair segregation laws:

   a. Linda Brown   b. Rose Duchesne   c. Anne Pellowski

Draw lines to match the state names with their capitals.

9. New York   Pierre

10. New Jersey   Lincoln

11. Pennsylvania   Bismarck

12. Illinois   St. Paul

13. Indiana   Springfield

14. Michigan   Topeka

15. Ohio   Albany

16. Wisconsin   Indianapolis

17. Iowa   Madison

18. Kansas   Lansing

19. Minnesota   Jefferson City

20. Missouri   Des Moines

21. Nebraska   Trenton

22. North Dakota   Columbus

23. South Dakota   Harrisburg

Review/Test

Northeastern & Midwestern Regions Map Test

Write the names of the states and their capitals on the correct states.

Southern Region
SOUTH ATLANTIC

Lessons Alive!

Georgia
Destruction and Reconstruction
- Some Civil War battles destroyed whole cities in the South. Atlanta, Georgia was burned almost completely to the ground when Union General Sherman attacked the city. Nearly all the businesses, hospitals, schools, stores, and homes were destroyed. People who had lived and worked in these places now had no homes, no jobs. Where would people live? How could children go to school? Where could the sick and injured go for treatment? Where could they find food and, if they found it, how could they buy it? They had no jobs, and no money.
- Reconstruction, or the rebuilding, of Atlanta and other southern cities and towns damaged by war, took many years. In the meantime, the South suffered terribly. Imagine that your town or city was heavily damaged during the Civil War. Drive through your town or community (or page through the phone book Yellow Pages) and make a list of the hospitals, businesses, and schools. Now cross off nine out of every ten buildings listed. (This is about the percentage of buildings lost in Atlanta.) How would the loss of these services affect your community? How might you, as a Catholic, have practiced the Corporal and Spiritual Works of Mercy if you had lived in a city damaged by the Civil War?

Florida
God's Creation
- The Florida Everglades, one of the largest swamps in the world, is filled with snakes, turtles, manatees, panthers, alligators, and more. Unusual plants also grow in the Everglades. "Explore" the Everglades using a library DVD or online videos.
- Explore in your own backyard. How many different animals and plants can you find just outside your door? Even if you live in the city, you might be surprised at the variety in God's creation. Perhaps set a time limit and see who can record the greatest number of different plants, animals, and insects in that time.

Virginia
God and Country
- Arlington National Cemetery honors soldiers from every American conflict. Think of a way that you can honor veterans—those who have died and especially those who are still living.
- Pope Pius XI kept a copy of Frank Parater's letter to comfort him in times of difficulty. Even those with the strongest faith need strengthening! Like Frank Parater, write a letter that will reassure someone of your prayers and of God's faithfulness, a letter that will strengthen someone's faith, a letter that they can keep for times of trial. Write this letter to your mom, dad, brother, or sister.

Maryland
God and Country
- Our national anthem, "The Star-Spangled Banner," reflects both love of God and love of country. Memorize the first and fourth verses. (This fourth verse is the origin of "In God We Trust.")

> *Oh! thus be it ever, when freemen shall stand*
> > *Between their loved home and the war's desolation!*
> *Blest with victory and peace, may the heav'n-rescued land*
> > *Praise the Power that hath made and preserved us a nation.*
> *Then conquer we must, when our cause it is just,*
> *And this be our motto: "In God is our trust."*
> > *And the star-spangled banner in triumph shall wave*
> > *O'er the land of the free and the home of the brave!*

Did you know that it is proper always, always to stand when you hear the national anthem? And, if the flag is present when the anthem is played, to salute it by placing your right hand over your heart?

- Charles Carroll was not an "official" church representative like a priest, but the way he lived his life as a Catholic inspired many to see Catholics more favorably. Some think it is only the job of priests or religious to be witnesses to the Faith, but we are all called to live Christ-like lives, to be Christ to the world. Think of tasks that you can do each day to quietly live out your Catholic faith in your day-to-day life, to be a witness to God's love to all those you meet.

Washington, D.C.
- Washington, D.C., our nation's capital, is home to the *federal* government, the government of the whole nation. Write a letter to the president or to your congressmen.

North and South Carolinas
Mysteries; God and Country
- What do you think happened to the people who lived in Roanoke, the "Lost Colony"? Write a story "solving" the mystery.
- Imagine that you were a Union soldier at Fort Sumter when it was fired upon, and when its flag was lowered in surrender. Now, think of the rejoicing when the Civil War ended and we were again "one nation, under God, indivisible." Memorize the Pledge of Allegiance that we say when we salute the flag. Find the meanings of: republic, indivisible, liberty, justice, allegiance.

> *I pledge allegiance to the flag of the United States of America, and to the republic for which it stands, one nation under God, indivisible, with liberty and justice for all.*

The Southern Region

1. There were many differences between northern and southern states. The North's economy depended on .... , while the South relied more on ....

2. Slaves worked on huge farms called ....

3. Eventually, the southern states wanted to leave, or .... from, the Union.

4. States that seceded, or left, the Union tried to form a new country called ....

5. This sad separation of our United States led to which war?
   ....

6. Even the president's family was torn by this sad war. Who was the president during this war?
   ....

7. The process of rebuilding the South was called ....

8. The Thirteenth Amendment to the Constitution made .... illegal forever.

9. On a separate piece of paper, give at least two examples from "The Southern Region" that tell how families and the country were torn apart during the Civil War.

Put on your thinking cap!

Think of at least two ways that the history of our country might have been different if there had never been a Civil War. Would your life have been different? In what way? Write out your ideas on the same piece of paper you used to answer #9.

Southern Region—South Atlantic

Florida, Maryland, and Virginia

1. Who explored Florida while looking for the Fountain of Youth?

   ....

2. What is the oldest permanent European settlement in North America?

   ....

3. What is the name of Florida's famous swamp?

   ....

4. This Catholic worked for King Charles I of England, who gave him the land that would become Maryland. Who was this man?

   ....

5. A special law declared that all Christians in Maryland had to be treated equally. What was the name of this law?

   ....

6. Who was the only Catholic to sign the Declaration of Independence?

   ....

7. What did Francis Scott Key write during the War of 1812 as he watched the British attack Fort McHenry?

   ....

8. When did Captain John Smith found the first permanent English settlement in Virginia?

   ....

9. What was the name of the settlement that Smith founded?
   ....

10. Which Powhatan princess saved John Smith's life?
    ....

11. Who said, "Give me liberty or give me death!"?
    ....

12. Who was our country's very first president?
    ....

13. Who was the author of the Declaration of Independence?
    ....

14. What was the name of the Virginian who led the Confederate army?
    ....

Maps and Caps

The South Atlantic states are:

- **Delaware**
- **Florida**
- **Georgia**
- **Maryland**
- **North Carolina**
- **South Carolina**
- **Virginia**
- **West Virginia**
- **Washington, District of Columbia** (which isn't really a state, but is instead our nation's capital!)

Write the names on the correct states. Research and find the capitals of the states and write their names in as well.

Draw and label a tiny star to mark the location of Washington, D.C.

Now find out where the Appalachian Mountains are located, and draw them across your map, too.

Make a hand-drawn copy of this map. In pencil, write in tiny, tiny letters the state and capital names on your hand-drawn map, too. How quickly can you memorize the states and their capitals?

Southern Region—South Atlantic

More South Atlantic States

1. What was the name of the machine that made the processing of cotton faster?
   ....

2. Who was forced to pick the cotton that was used to make cloth?
   ....

3. During the Civil War, which Union general marched to the city of Atlanta and burned it to the ground?
   ....

4. Name the great civil rights leader who was born in Atlanta.
   ....

5. At first, North and South Carolina were one big colony called what?
   ....

6. James Hoban was a gifted architect who designed which famous house?
   ....

7. Who donated the land for the "District of Columbia"?
   ....

8. The first shots of the Civil War were fired when troops from South Carolina attacked Union troops who were staying where?
   ....

9. Who was president of the United States during the Civil War?
   ....

10. What is the name of our nation's capital?

   ....

11. In the name of our nation's capital, what do the letters "D.C." stand for?

   ....

12. In the first section of your text, you learned that our government is divided into three branches, and you learned what role each of these branches plays in our federal, or national, government.

Match these terms:

executive branch   Congress

legislative branch   Supreme Court

judicial branch   president

(If you need to, you may look back in your textbook to "America's System of Government," page 10.)

Learning the States:

Can you identify the states and their capitals yet? Time to practice! Give someone your map and have them test you. How did you do?

Time to Grab Maps and Thinking Caps!

Map Challenge

Carefully study the map for this region on page 53. Do you have the states and capitals memorized? Good! Get a fresh piece of paper, turn the map over, and draw from memory the map with all the states in this region. Label the state names and capitals. When you are done, compare your map with the workbook map. How did you do? (You will soon be tested on the states and their capitals.) If your map isn't quite right, re-draw it now.

Mapping the Economy

Delaware, Florida, Georgia, Maryland, North and South Carolina, Virginia, West Virginia, Washington, D.C.

Grab your hand-drawn map, and put on your thinking cap! Now, turn to these states in your textbook. What types of factory goods are produced in these states? Starting with the first state, find at least two products that are manufactured for each state. Draw small symbols or pictures of these products on your map, on the states where they are manufactured.

What else do the people of these states produce for the state's economy? Pick two more products for each state and draw those on your map as well. Look for things that make up an economy by providing jobs, and things that people buy and sell. Be sure to include natural resources!

Put on Those Thinking Caps

Turn back to the page titled "South Atlantic Region" in your textbook, page 105. Read this page to find out about the climate, weather, and geography, or the type of land found in this region. Is the region mostly hot, bare deserts, or does it have mountains covered with trees? Is it near the ocean, or miles and miles away from any water?

On a separate piece of paper, write the name of the region. Then write the words that you have found that tell about climate, weather, and geography.

In your map assignment, you discovered and drew symbols of jobs and industry that make up this region's economy. With this information about the economy, climate, and geography, why do you think that this region has the jobs that it does? Do the people who live in the state make good use of the land, water, and natural resources that God has provided?

Now, write a sentence or two telling why the jobs and climate, geography, and natural resources fit so well together.

Southern Region
EAST & WEST SOUTH-CENTRAL

Lessons Alive!

Alabama
Faith, Perseverance, and Hard Work Benefit Society
- George Washington Carver, born a slave and raised in poverty, worked hard to get an education. He could have been resentful, but instead he used the gifts that God gave him to benefit the South's economy and people. Carver's experiments developed hundreds of new products made with peanuts and sweet potatoes, which could be grown on southern farms. A devout Christian, Carver often gave God credit for his success. Find out more about this remarkable man.
- Make a meal based on sweet potatoes and foods made with peanuts.
- Helen Keller and Mother Angelica both struggled with disabilities. They could have given up and felt sorry for themselves. Both persevered and made great contributions to society. (In what ways has EWTN changed the lives of people all over the world?) Pick one of these amazing women and find out more about her life. (For fun, you might watch *"The Miracle Worker"* [1962] or record a video of your own "TV program" that communicates a message of Faith.)

Kentucky
- Listen to some bluegrass music! Bill Monroe is considered a master.

Louisiana
The *Real* Mardi Gras
- Emphasize the true religious aspect of "Fat Tuesday," which involved using up all the fat in the house before the beginning of Lenten penance. ("Carnival" comes from the Latin words *carnis + vale* or literally, "meat + good-bye"!)
- In honor of Louisiana's French and Cajun culture, learn a few French words and make some gumbo or jambalaya.
- Hurricanes frequently hit this region. Can you think of a way to help hurricane victims, or the victims of another natural disaster?

Oklahoma
- The government broke its promise that Oklahoma would be for Native American use for all time. Why is it important for our country to keep its promises? (It usually does.) Why is it important for each of us to keep our promises?
- Find out about the Native American reservations that exist in more than twenty states. Is there a reservation near you?

Texas
- The Alamo began its existence as a Spanish mission. Find out more about this mission and the role it played in American history. There are several film adaptations of "The Alamo," some more faithful than others.

Maps and Caps

The East South-Central states are:

- **Alabama**
- **Kentucky**
- **Mississippi**
- **Tennessee**

The West South-Central states are:

- **Arkansas**
- **Louisiana**
- **Oklahoma**
- **Texas**

Write the names on the correct states. Research and find the capitals of the states and write their names in as well.

Now make a hand-drawn copy of this map. In pencil, write in tiny, tiny letters the state and capital names on your hand-drawn map, too.

How quickly can you memorize the states and their capitals?

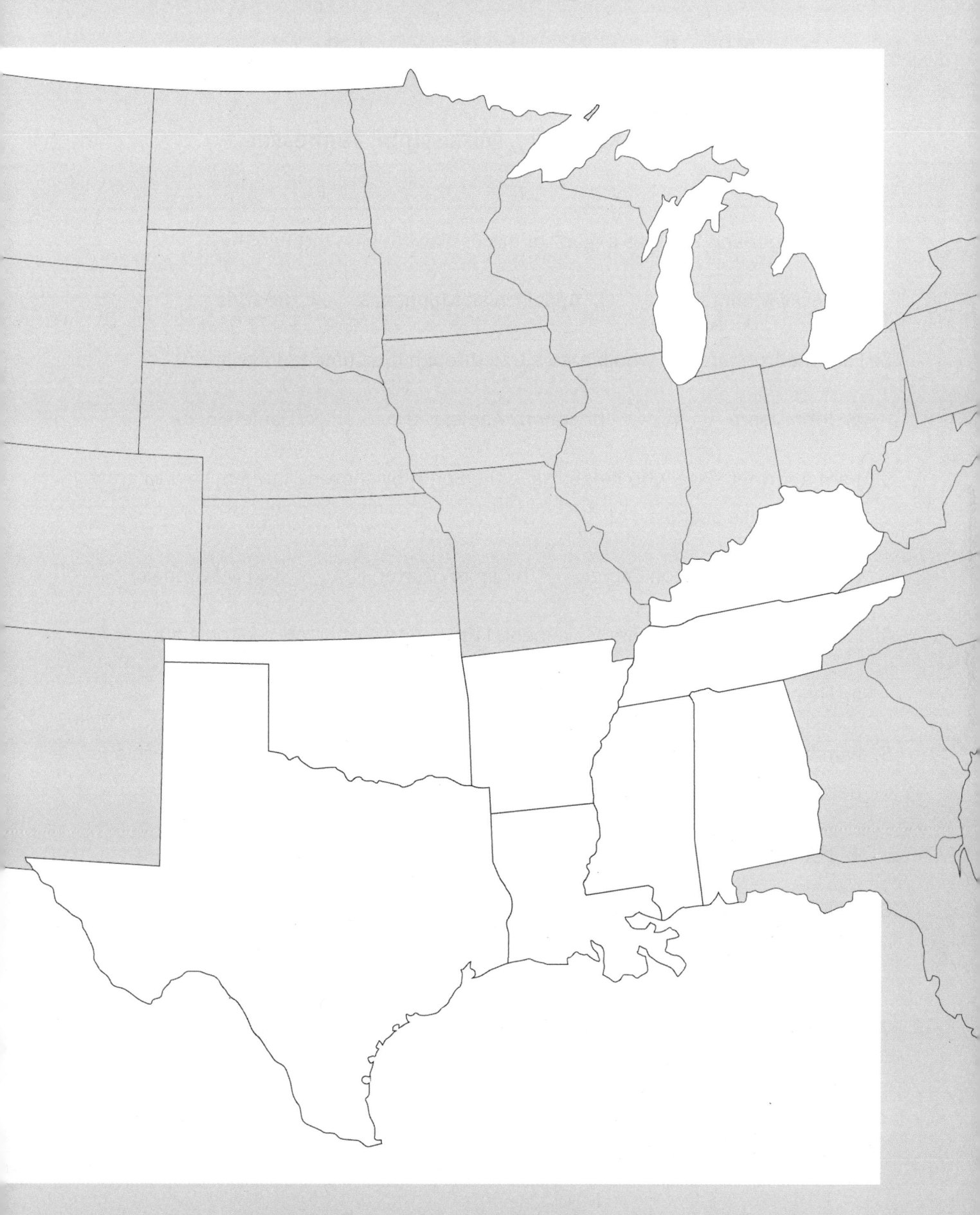

Southern Region—East & West South-Central

The East South-Central Region

Alabama, Kentucky, Mississippi, Tennessee

1. The Cumberland Gap was a "gap" or easier place to pass through the

    a. Rocky Mountains   b. Appalachian Mountains   c. Red Sea

2. I am the frontiersman who blazed a trail through the Cumberland Gap!

    a. John Deere   b. Johnny Appleseed   c. Daniel Boone

3. I am a former slave who helped save the South by showing farmers how to grow new crops like peanuts.

    a. George Washington Carver   b. Jimmy Carter   c. Old MacDonald

4. I am part of the Civil Rights Movement. I refused to give up my seat on a bus.

    a. Helen Keller   b. Rosa Parks   c. Jesse Owens

5. I am blind and deaf but, using the gifts God gave me, I graduated from college and became a famous author.

    a. Helen Keller   b. Rosa Parks   c. Jesse Owens

6. Using the gifts God gave me, I became a nun. I started a Catholic television network.

    a. Helen Keller   b. Mother Teresa   c. Mother Angelica

7. I am the American Civil War president who was born in Kentucky.

    a. Jefferson Davis   b. George Washington   c. Abraham Lincoln

8. I am the Confederate Civil War president who was also born in Kentucky.

   a. Jefferson Davis   b. George Washington   c. Abraham Lincoln

9. I am a Spanish explorer who explored the southern states that you now study.

   a. Hernando de Soto   b. Christopher Columbus   c. Zorro

10. I am a Cherokee who developed an alphabet for the Cherokee language.

    a. Hernando de Soto   b. Sitting Bull   c. Sequoyah

Bonus point:

How many different countries claimed Alabama before it became a state?

The West South-Central Region

Arkansas, Louisiana, Oklahoma, Texas

1. I, along with other French Catholics, was kicked out of Canada by the British. I fled to Louisiana so I could practice my Faith in peace. I am
   a. an Acadian
   b. a Creole
   c. a gumbo

2. I am a student who wanted only to go to the high school of my choice, but was turned away because of my race. I was one of the
   a. High School Nine
   b. High Fives
   c. Little Rock Nine

3. I am a Cherokee who barely survived a forced march from my home in the South all the way to Oklahoma. This forced march was called
   a. the Trail of Tears
   b. the Chisolm Trail
   c. the Oregon Trail

4. In the 1930s, a fierce drought dried up the soil and destroyed many farms. The area affected by this drought was called
   a. the Rose Bowl
   b. Mud Wrestling
   c. the Dust Bowl

5. Six different countries have flown their flags over me. I am the state of
   a. Confusion
   b. Arkansas
   c. Texas

6. In 1822, when Mexico invited American settlement to what became Texas, I led 297 Americans to start the first settlement. The state capital of Texas is named after me. I am
   a. Davy Crockett
   b. Stephen Austin
   c. Sheriff Woody

7. I am an American folk hero who fought to defend the Alamo.
   a. Davy Crockett
   b. Stephen Austin
   c. Sheriff Woody

8. Our second-largest state is
   a. Rhode Island
   b. Texas
   c. Alaska

Learning the States:
Can you identify the states and their capitals yet? Time to practice! Give someone your map and have them test you. How did you do?

Time to Grab Maps and Thinking Caps!

Map Challenge

Carefully study the map for this region on page 59. Do you have the states and capitals memorized? Good! Get a fresh piece of paper, turn the map over, and draw from memory the map with all the states in this region. Label the state names and capitals. When you are done, compare your map with the workbook map. How did you do? (You will soon be tested on the states and their capitals.) If your map isn't quite right, re-draw it now.

Mapping the Economy
Alabama, Kentucky, Mississippi, Tennessee, Arkansas, Louisiana, Oklahoma, Texas

Grab your hand-drawn map, and put on your thinking cap! Now, turn to these states in your textbook. What types of factory goods are produced in these states? Starting with the first state, find at least two products that are manufactured for each state. Draw small symbols or pictures of these products on your map, on the states where they are manufactured.

What else do the people of these states produce for the state's economy? Pick two more products for each state and draw those on your map as well. Look for things that make up an economy by providing jobs, and things that people buy and sell. Be sure to include natural resources!

Put on Those Thinking Caps

In your textbook, turn back to the pages titled "East South-Central Region" and then "West South-Central Region," pages 132 and 142. Read these pages to find out about the climate, weather, and geography, or the type of land found in these regions. Are the regions mostly hot, bare deserts, or do they have mountains covered with trees? Are they near the ocean, or miles and miles away from any water?

On a separate piece of paper, write the names of the regions. Then write the words that you have found that tell about climate, weather, and geography.

In your map assignment, you discovered and drew symbols of jobs and industry that make up this region's economy. With this information about the economy, climate, and geography, why do you think that this region has the jobs that it does? Do the people who live in these states make good use of the land, water, and natural resources that God has provided?

Now, write a sentence or two telling why the jobs and climate, geography, and natural resources fit so well together.

Southern Region—East & West South-Central

The Southern Region Review/Test

1. In the South, slaves worked on huge farms called ....

2. The southern states seceded, or left the Union, to start a "country" called the
   a. United States of America   b. Texas   c. Confederate States of America

3. The war between the states was called the ....

4. Which man was President of the United States during this terrible war?
   a. Jefferson Davis   b. Abraham Lincoln   c. George Washington

5. Which man was President of the Confederate States of America?
   a. Jefferson Davis   b. Abraham Lincoln   c. George Washington

6. Which amendment to the Constitution made slavery illegal?
   a. Thirteenth Amendment   b. Civil Rights Amendment   c. First Amendment

7. The name of the great civil rights leader who was born in Atlanta:
   a. Davy Crockett   b. Mother Angelica   c. Martin Luther King, Jr.

8. Our nation's capital is ....

9. The frontiersman who blazed a trail through the Cumberland Gap:
   a. Daniel Boone   b. Davy Crockett   c. Stephen Austin

10. In the 1930s, a fierce drought dried up the soil and destroyed many farms. The area affected by this drought was called ....

11. Which man was the first President of the United States of America?
    a. Jefferson Davis   b. Abraham Lincoln   c. George Washington

Review/Test

Draw lines to match the state names with their capitals.

12. Delaware	Raleigh

13. Florida	Austin

14. Georgia	Richmond

15. Maryland	Charleston

16. North Carolina	Frankfort

17. South Carolina	Nashville

18. Virginia	Oklahoma City

19. West Virginia	Atlanta

20. Alabama	Jackson

21. Kentucky	Little Rock

22. Mississippi	Baton Rouge

23. Tennessee	Montgomery

24. Arkansas	Columbia

25. Louisiana	Annapolis

26. Oklahoma	Dover

27. Texas	Tallahassee

Review/Test

The Southern Region Map Test

Write the names of the states and their capitals on the correct states.

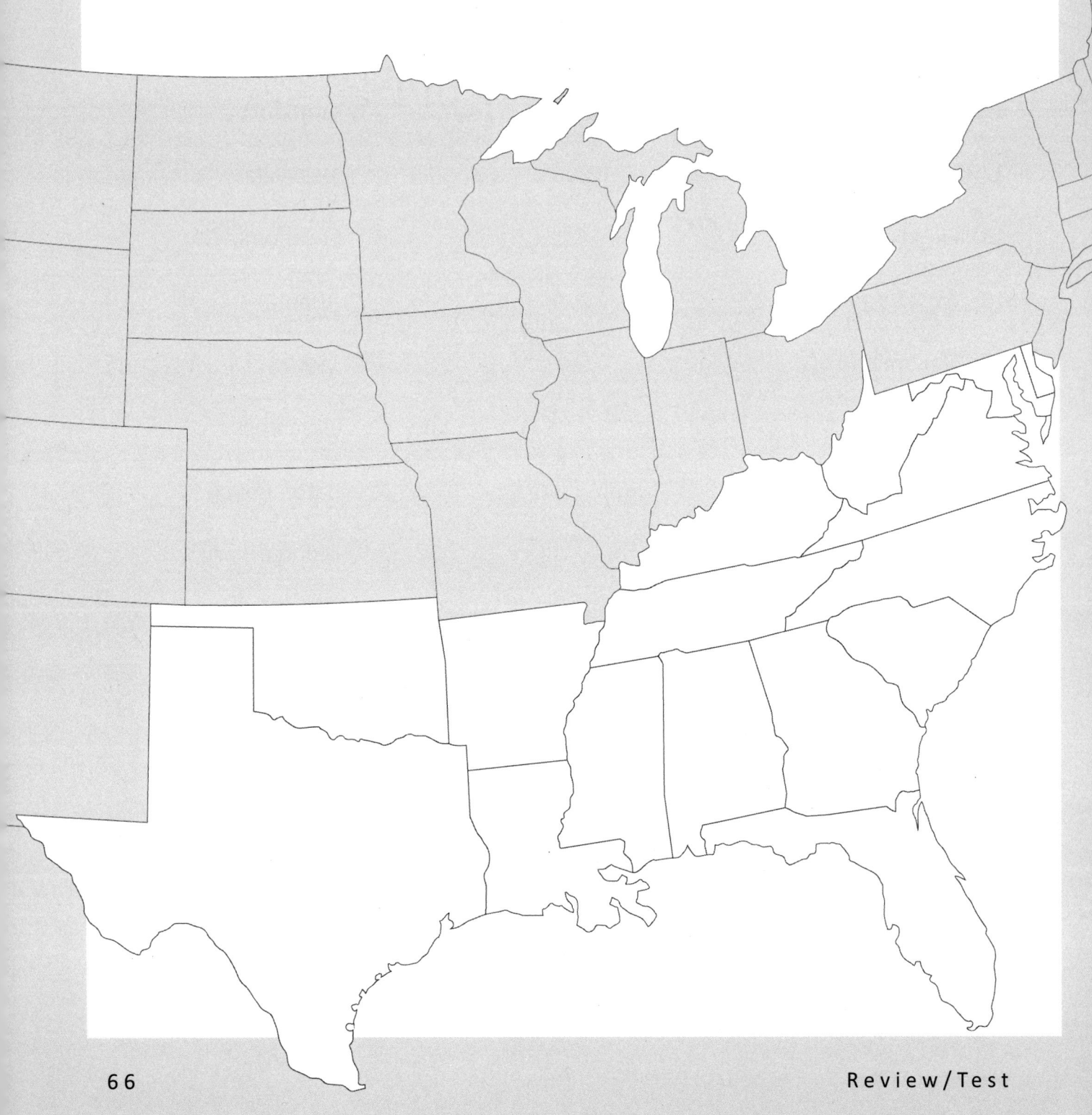

Review/Test

Western Region
MOUNTAIN

Lessons Alive!

Arizona
Culture
- Mexican-American culture has brought us nopales, or nopalitos, from the prickly-pear cactus (also known as nopal cactus). The cactus "leaves," with the sharp spines cut off, are nutritious and tasty. Find nopales in your grocery store, fresh or canned, and prepare a Mexican dish. Look for prickly-pear cactus at a local nursery and grow your own!
- Find out more about Navajo Code Talkers, who were responsible for many American victories in World War II. These hero-soldiers were members of the Navajo Nation (which covers parts of Arizona and other southwestern states). Code Talkers made up secret codes using their native language; for example, the code word for submarine was "besh-lo," or "iron fish." When enemy soldiers read or heard the messages, they couldn't understand them.
- Early Christians, when persecuted for their beliefs, also used "code symbols" to share their Faith. Make up a secret symbol-code that you could use to tell people about Our Lord and His Church!

Colorado
God and Country
- After gazing at the majestic view from Pike's Peak, Katherine Lee Bates wrote "America the Beautiful." This song reflects both love of God and love of country. Can you memorize these verses?

O beautiful for spacious skies,
For amber waves of grain,
For purple mountain majesties
Above the fruited plain!
America! America!
God shed his grace on thee
And crown thy good with brotherhood
From sea to shining sea!

O beautiful for pilgrim feet
Whose stern impassioned stress
A thoroughfare of freedom beat
Across the wilderness!
America! America!
God mend thine every flaw,
Confirm thy soul in self-control,
Thy liberty in law!

O beautiful for heroes proved
In liberating strife.
Who more than self their country loved
And mercy more than life!
America! America!
May God thy gold refine
Till all success be nobleness
And every gain divine!

Idaho
Economy
- Idaho is famous for its potatoes. Prepare a meal centered around the lowly potato. Will you serve potato soup and potato bread, or potato pancakes and mashed potato cookies?

Montana

Cowboy Culture

- Go to a rodeo, or check out a DVD on rodeos, roping, and bull riding.

- Get a rope and learn how to make and use a lasso.

- Find a riding stable near you and go horseback riding, or take riding lessons.

New Mexico

Culture

- Prepare a Mexican fiesta! Make your own piñata from paper mache. *(https://www.wikihow.com/Make-a-Pinata)* If you are doing this activity in late winter or early spring, you might include a dish made with nopal cactus, which is traditionally served during Lent. Find a recording of mariachi music to play during your festival.

- Learn a few words of Spanish.

- Assist at a Spanish-language Mass near you. Can you learn some of the Spanish-language hymns in the missalette? (Even if you don't have a Spanish-language Mass nearby, you can still learn some of these hymns. Look in the back of your missalette!)

Utah

- Utah's Philo Farnsworth invented the television. In his honor, celebrate what life was like *before* his invention; unplug the television for a week. (Now you have more time to create your own invention.)

- Make a list of ways that you think television has made our society better. Now make a list of ways that television has harmed our society. Sometimes things aren't good or bad in themselves, but in the way they are used. As Christians, we want to use all things for good, in ways that will make us better people and more faithful followers of our Lord and Savior, Jesus Christ. A good way to decide whether something is good or not is to remember this scripture: ". . . whatever you do, do all to the glory of God." 1 Cor. 10:31. Does the program or activity in some way give glory to God?

Maps and Caps

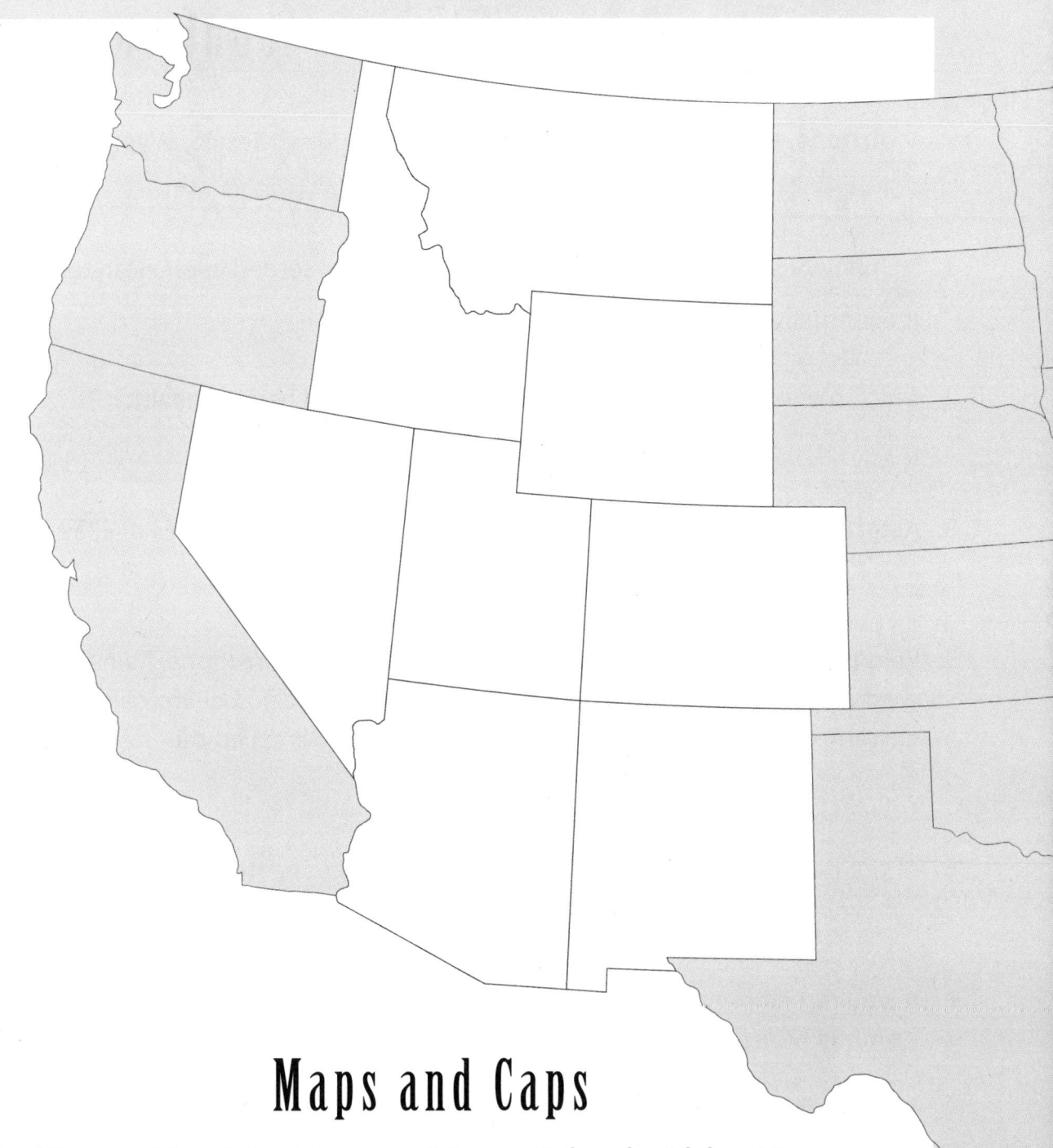

The Western Mountain states are: **Arizona, Colorado, Idaho, Montana, Nevada, New Mexico, Wyoming, Utah.** Write the names on the correct states. Research and find the capitals of the states and write their names in as well.

Now make a hand-drawn copy of this map. In pencil, write in tiny, tiny letters the state and capital names on your hand-drawn map, too.

How quickly can you memorize the states and their capitals?

Western Region — Mountain

The Western Region: Mountain

Arizona, Colorado, Idaho, Montana, Nevada, New Mexico, Wyoming, Utah

1. So many Americans followed the Santa Fe Trail and settled in Mexican territory that it eventually became the cause of the ....

2. Which religious sister nursed the outlaw Billy the Kid back to health?

   ....

3. Apartment-like homes that Native Americans built into the sides of cliffs are called

   ....

4. Rain falling on Rocky Mountain peaks "splits" in two directions. Rain falling on the west side of the peaks eventually drains into the Pacific Ocean; rain falling on the eastern side drains toward the Atlantic. This "split" is called the

   ....

5. At the battle of Little Big Horn, Custer's troops were beaten by

   .... and ....

6. Do you remember which amendment to the Constitution made slavery illegal? Write its name here:

   ....

7. Transportation across the United States improved significantly when shorter rail lines were finally joined into one railroad system that could travel all the way across the United States. This new system was called the

   ....

8. This state was the first to elect a female governor:

   ....

Time to Grab Maps and Thinking Caps!

Map Challenge

Carefully study the map for this region on page 69. Do you have the states and capitals memorized? Good! Get a fresh piece of paper, turn the map over, and draw from memory the map with all the states in this region. Label the state names and capitals. When you are done, compare your map with the workbook map. How did you do? (You will soon be tested on the states and their capitals.) If your map isn't quite right, re-draw it now.

Mapping the Economy

Arizona, Colorado, Idaho, Montana, Nevada, New Mexico, Wyoming, Utah

Grab your hand-drawn map, and put on your thinking cap! Now, turn to these states in your textbook. What types of factory goods are produced in these states? Starting with the first state, find at least two products that are manufactured for each state. Draw small symbols or pictures of these products on your map, on the states where they are manufactured.

What else do the people of these states produce for the state's economy? Pick two more products for each state and draw those on your map as well. Look for things that make up an economy by providing jobs, and things that people buy and sell. Be sure to include natural resources!

Put on Those Thinking Caps

Turn back to the page titled "Mountain Region" in your textbook, page 157. Read this page to find out about the climate, weather, and geography, or the type of land found in this region. Is the region mostly hot, bare deserts, or does it have mountains covered with trees? Is it near the ocean, or miles and miles away from any water?

On a separate piece of paper, write the name of the region. Then write the words that you have found that tell about climate, weather, and geography.

In your map assignment, you discovered and drew symbols of jobs and industry that make up this region's economy. With this information about the economy, climate, and geography, why do you think that this region has the jobs that it does? Do the people who live in the state make good use of the land, water, and natural resources that God has provided?

Now, write a sentence or two telling why the jobs and climate, geography, and natural resources fit so well together.

Western Region — Mountain

Western Region
PACIFIC

Lessons Alive!

California

Faith and Economy

- St. Junipero Serra and other Spanish missionaries founded twenty-one missions in California. Towns and cities developed from the missions. Many of these cities took the names of the missions. Look at a map of California and see how many you can find. (Hint: Most of the names start with "San" or "Santa," which means "saint" or "holy" in Spanish.)

- Citrus crops like lemons, limes, and oranges make up an important part of California's economy. You very likely have eaten citrus fruits grown in California, but do you know who first planted citrus trees in California? Spanish missionaries! So our Holy Faith is linked even to the economy of California. Do you suppose that St. Serra could have imagined that his simple orchards and gardens would feed not only those who lived at the missions, but would be the "first fruits" of farm products that would feed generations of people in the United States and beyond? How much little acts of faithfulness can grow! What little acts of faithfulness can you "plant" that may spread to generations beyond?

- Make a salad with citrus fruits, or an orange smoothie for lunch!

Alaska

Culture and Economy

- Nalukataq is an Inupiaq Eskimo celebration of thanksgiving for a good whaling season. This celebration wouldn't be complete without the "blanket toss," in which a sort of "trampoline" is made using a stretched "blanket" made of animal skins. One person stands on the "blanket," while a crowd gathers around, jerking on the edge of the "blanket" to throw the person into the air. The person being tossed continues his turn as long as he can stay upright. Perhaps, with your teacher's permission, you can try this with an old blanket and a group of friends.

- Alaska is famous for its Kodiak bears, which can reach a standing height of eight feet tall. Measure the height of a doorway in your house. Would the bear fit through the door without having to "duck"?

- In the late summer and fall, Kodiak bears feast on salmon they catch in Alaska's beautiful rivers. Make a meal fit for a bear, and for people, too: prepare a recipe that includes Alaskan salmon, fresh, frozen, or canned.

Hawaii

Culture

- Hawaii is famous for welcoming visitors with the "lei," a delicate "necklace" made from flowers. Try your hand at making a lei, either from real or home-made paper flowers. (Patterns and directions are available online.)

Oregon

Pioneer History

- Do you remember reading about "schooners," Maine's 18th-century sailing ships that carried passengers and goods over the Atlantic Ocean? "Prairie Schooners" was the nickname given to covered wagons that carried pioneers across grassy prairies to Oregon. The wagon bed of a Prairie Schooner measured 4 ft. by 12 ft. Measure out that area in your living room. In this space, pioneers packed everything they would take with them to begin a new life in Oregon, including food for the five-month trip across the country. Not many household belongings would fit after their supplies were packed. Pretend that you are going to travel the Oregon Trail. What would you take with you? Do you think you can fit all your belongings in? What would you leave behind?

    https://www.blm.gov/sites/blm.gov/files/learn_interp_nhotic_edguide.pdf —see Activity #4

- Camp out under the stars! Many pioneers on the trail slept on the ground under the wagon as there simply wasn't room for everyone inside. Would you like to camp out for five months as the pioneers did?

Washington

Culture

- Early explorers and settlers to the Northwest saw totem poles in native villages. On these poles were carved images that often "told" the story of native legends. With your teacher's permission, design a totem with two figures or symbols that would "tell a story" from the life of Our Lord and then carve them from rectangular bars of soft, white soap. Leave the ends of the bars flat so when you are done, the carvings can be "stacked" on one another. Break a toothpick in half. Carefully make a toothpick-size hole in the top and bottom of the "soap totem" pieces you want to join. Stick the half-toothpick in one piece, then fit the second soap piece on the other end of the toothpick, thus joining the pieces.

U.S. Territories

Faith and Culture

- Find on a map the U.S. Territories of Guam and Puerto Rico. In which seas or oceans are these islands found? What do these far-flung territories have in common?

- Most residents of these islands share the Catholic—universal—Faith and traditions! Three Kings Day is celebrated on January 6th by many in Puerto Rico and Guam. These territories celebrate in somewhat different ways, but both honor the day when the Wise Men presented gifts to the Baby Jesus. Gifts are usually exchanged, and a special cake is made to honor the Wise Men. Make and decorate a cake to look like a King's crown.

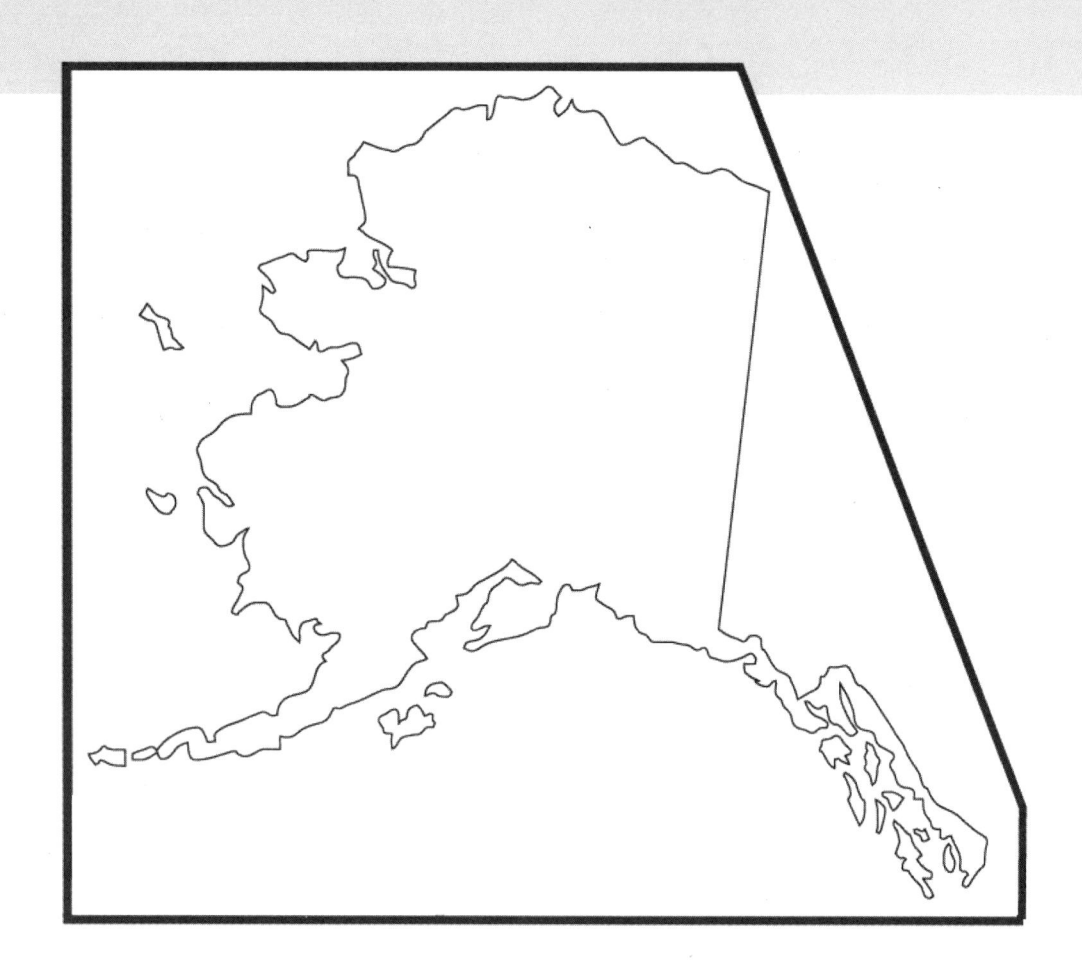

Maps and Caps

The Western Pacific states are: **Alaska, California, Hawaii, Oregon, Washington.**

Write the names on the correct states. Research and find the capitals of the states and write their names in as well.

Now make a hand-drawn copy of this map. In pencil, write in tiny, tiny letters the state and capital names on your hand-drawn map, too.

How quickly can you memorize the states and their capitals?

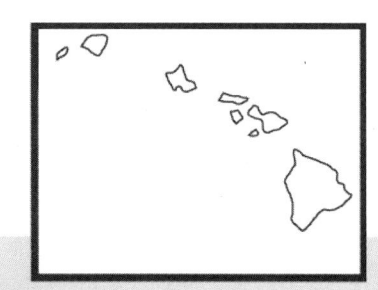

Western Region—Pacific

Western Region: Pacific

Western Region—Pacific

The Western Region: Pacific

Read the sentences below. Look for the "5 W's."

Who   (did)What   When   Where   Why

1. Who were the first Europeans to reach Alaska? ....

2. When did these first Europeans start fur-trading settlements in Alaska? ....

3. What did Joe Juneau discover in Alaska? ....

4. Why did the "forty-niners" rush to California? ....
....

5. Who was the Spanish priest that began missions for the Native Americans of California?
....

6. Where did Fr. Damien serve lepers? ....

7. Which lines on a map or globe measure distances from north to south?
....

8. Which lines on a map or globe measure distances from east to west?
....

9. What are the five largest U.S. Territories?
....
....

Learning the States:

Can you identify the states and their capitals yet? Time to practice! Give someone your map and have them test you. How did you do?

Time to Grab Maps and Thinking Caps!

Map Challenge

Carefully study the map for this region on pages 74-75. Do you have the states and capitals memorized? Good! Get a fresh piece of paper, turn the map over, and draw from memory the map with all the states in this region. Label the state names and capitals. When you are done, compare your map with the workbook map. How did you do? (You will soon be tested on the states and their capitals.) If your map isn't quite right, re-draw it now.

Mapping the Economy

Alaska, California, Hawaii, Oregon, Washington

Grab your hand-drawn map, and put on your thinking cap! Now, turn to these states in your textbook. What types of factory goods are produced in these states? Starting with the first state, find at least two products that are manufactured for each state. Draw small symbols or pictures of these products on your map, on the states where they are manufactured.

What else do the people of these states produce for the state's economy? Pick two more products for each state and draw those on your map as well. Look for things that make up an economy by providing jobs, and things that people buy and sell. Be sure to include natural resources!

Put on Those Thinking Caps

Turn back to the page titled "Pacific Region" in your textbook, page 180. Read this page to find out about the climate, weather, and geography, or the type of land found in this region. Is the region mostly hot, bare deserts, or does it have mountains covered with trees? Is it near the ocean, or miles and miles away from any water?

On a separate piece of paper, write the name of the region. Then write the words that you have found that tell about climate, weather, and geography.

In your map assignment, you discovered and drew symbols of jobs and industry that make up this region's economy. With this information about the economy, climate, and geography, why do you think that this region has the jobs that it does? Do the people who live in the state make good use of the land, water, and natural resources that God has provided?

Now, write a sentence or two telling why the jobs and climate, geography, and natural resources fit so well together.

Western Region—Pacific

"5 W's": Making Sense and Sentences

Turn to the "California Catholic Heritage" page in your textbook, pages 190-191. These "5 W's" are from paragraphs #5, 6, and 7 on the first and second pages.

Who: Fr. Junipero Serra

(did) What: traveled through Upper California on foot

When: in 1769

Where: to San Diego

Why: to start a series of nine missions among the Native Americans

Now let's turn the "5 W's" into a few simple sentences.

> In 1769, Fr. Junipero Serra traveled through Upper California on foot, to start a series of missions. His first mission, built at San Diego, served Native Americans living in the region. This was the first of nine missions that Father Serra founded in California.

Notice that this new paragraph isn't worded exactly the same as the text. However, this new paragraph "summarizes," or tells the same general information in fewer words.

Now, it's your turn! Turn to the "A Nation Built by Immigrants" sidebar page which follows "Hawaii" in your textbook, page 195. Find the "5 W's." Write them below. Then, on a separate sheet, make a sentence for each "W." As in the exercise above, your wording will not be the same as the book's wording. Instead, it will give the same general information in your own words.

Who is the person discussed in this selection?

....

....

....

(did) What is mentioned in the selection about this person?

....

....

....

When did the event or events happen?

....

....

....

Where did the event or events happen?

....

....

....

Why did the events happen?

....

....

....

Western Region—Pacific

The Western Region Review/Test

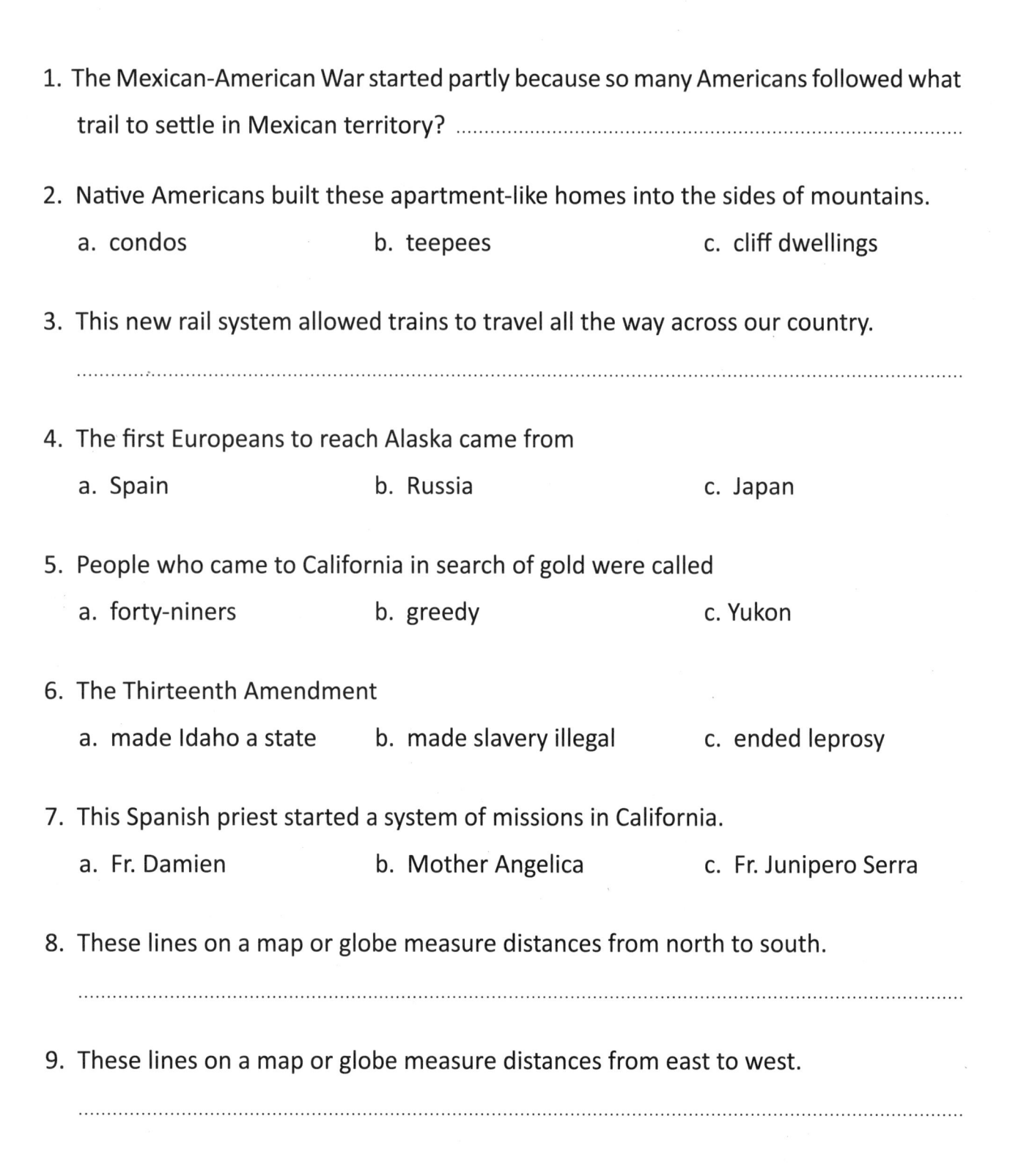

1. The Mexican-American War started partly because so many Americans followed what trail to settle in Mexican territory? ....

2. Native Americans built these apartment-like homes into the sides of mountains.
    a. condos
    b. teepees
    c. cliff dwellings

3. This new rail system allowed trains to travel all the way across our country.
   ....

4. The first Europeans to reach Alaska came from
    a. Spain
    b. Russia
    c. Japan

5. People who came to California in search of gold were called
    a. forty-niners
    b. greedy
    c. Yukon

6. The Thirteenth Amendment
    a. made Idaho a state
    b. made slavery illegal
    c. ended leprosy

7. This Spanish priest started a system of missions in California.
    a. Fr. Damien
    b. Mother Angelica
    c. Fr. Junipero Serra

8. These lines on a map or globe measure distances from north to south.
   ....

9. These lines on a map or globe measure distances from east to west.
   ....

10. On December 7, 1941, World War II began for America with the bombing of
   a. Pearl Harbor, Hawaii   b. Juneau, Alaska   c. Little Big Horn

Draw lines to match the state names with their capitals.

11. Alaska   Salt Lake City

12. Arizona   Santa Fe

13. Oregon   Honolulu

14. Nevada   Phoenix

15. Washington   Sacramento

16. Utah   Juneau

17. Hawaii   Carson City

18. New Mexico   Helena

19. Idaho   Cheyenne

20. California   Salem

21. Montana   Denver

22. Wyoming   Olympia

23. Colorado   Boise

The Western Region Map Test

Write the names of the states and their capitals on the correct states.

Learning about My State

Pre-tour and Prepping

You have now learned a bit about each of our fifty states, but there is so much more to discover! I hope you will keep your "detective cap" on, digging up yet more exciting true stories about these great United States. For the next nine weeks, however, you will examine more closely the sometimes surprising events and activities that shaped, and still affect, your own state.

Long before your parents or grandparents or great-grandparents were born, Native Americans lived in your state. What do you know about these ancient peoples?

You can find out by visiting places where these first residents lived. If you live in New Mexico, for example, you can visit the Gila and Puye Cliff Dwellings, where these ancient peoples lived long ago. How were their lives different from yours? How were they the same?

After a time, explorers, missionaries, and settlers came from Europe to explore, to spread the good news about Jesus, and to build a new life in your state. Who lived in your state long ago, hundreds of years before your parents or grandparents or great-grandparents were born? How can you find out?

A good place to begin the search for answers is in your state capitol, sometimes called a statehouse. The state capitol is the place where your state government is located. Just as the federal government has a Senate and House of Representatives, so too does your state government. People who have been elected to lead your state, such as your governor, senators, and representatives, work at the state capitol. Visit your state capitol, meet some of your senators and representatives, and explore the senate and house chambers where decisions are made about how you live in your state.

State capitols also have information about the history of your state. Often, capitol walls are covered with murals, or paintings, that tell the history of the state. Capitol guides give tours that teach about state history and government.

Capitol buildings also have museum stores or gift shops that are filled with books, DVDs, and other materials that tell the amazing story of your state. There are books for adults, and books for children; books about places to visit; and exciting stories of early peoples and settlers.

The very best way that you can begin your state study is with a visit to your state capitol. During your visit, you will begin to have your questions answered, and you can select and bring home materials that will make your state study exciting. Plan to begin your state study with such a visit. If you can do this at least a week or two before you begin the State Study unit in this book, so much the better.

If it simply isn't possible to visit your statehouse, virtual tours are available online. These tours are usually linked to your state capitol's website; by browsing the website you may also find and order materials about your state. Search online for "virtual tour [name of your state] capitol building."

When you studied social studies or history in the past, you may have used textbooks for most of your study. As you mature, or grow up in body, mind, and soul, you will begin to take more and more responsibility for finding information about topics outside of textbooks. This doesn't mean that textbooks are not valuable, or that you will no longer use them. Textbooks are a good starting point in learning.

But to really understand a subject, we often need to research, or search for materials about a subject, beyond the textbook. Your state study is a good time to learn research skills that you will use in later grades.

There are many places to find more information, including books from the library or bookstore; on the internet; watching DVDs; and visiting places where you can learn more about your subject.

Resources:

- As always, a set of encyclopedias is a valuable resource for information about individual states, including maps, state history, climate, industry, and much more.

- Your local library will have a good selection of books, encyclopedias, and DVDs with information about your state.

- Your state capitol museum/gift shop will have a good selection of books and DVDs as well.

- Auto travel clubs offer free state tour books to members; these books contain locations of museums and historical sites that you can visit.

- The internet offers a great number of sites that link to information about your state, from free outline maps to video clips of important events in your state history.

Links:
    https://awesomeamerica.com/
    https://www.factmonster.com/explore-all-fifty-us-states
    https://kids.nationalgeographic.com/geography/states
    https://www.ducksters.com/geography/usgeography.php

For your internet search box:

your state name + historical society	your state name + history online
your state name + historical museum	your state name + economy
your state name + natural resources	your state name + historical sites
your state name + historical landmarks	

If you haven't already done so, please gather the materials that you will use to research about your state now.

For this state study, you will need a 3-ring binder with a clear plastic cover and an inside pocket to hold papers that are not 3-hole-punched. This binder will store your state study projects and activities; it will become a permanent record of your state study.

State Study

Visiting the State Capitol

Please take a small notebook to record information on murals, statues, and other displays that you see inside and outside the capitol. What were the most exciting things that you learned in your visit? In the spaces below, write names of people and events, for you may read about them as you research your state's history. You may also use this information later to learn more about important people and events in your state.

People
....
....
....
....

Events
....
....
....
....

Other
....
....
....
....

Introduction to My State

State Study: Week One

In your textbook, *Our United States of America*, you have studied the different regions and states that make up our great nation. Just as our United States is made up of many states, each state is made up of neighborhoods, communities, and counties. You "belong" to a neighborhood, community, county, and state.

You have spent the last several months learning a bit about every state in our nation. Now you will begin nine weeks of research and hands-on projects to learn even more about your own state.

As the assignments and simple projects in this nine-week state study are completed, place them in your 3-ring binder. At the end of the nine weeks, you will have created your own, detailed state book. The information in this book may be used to make an oral presentation. The binder will be a permanent record of all the exciting things you have learned about your state's events, people, and places.

This nine-week course will also teach you writing tips that will be useful in writing assignments that you will have in coming years.

☆ Finding Information about My State ☆

You recently learned of *resources*, or places and books from which to gather information about your state. In the spaces below, tell which resources you will use to learn more about your state.

Which encyclopedia will you use? Write its title here:
....

Which books will you use? Write their titles here:
....
....
....
....

Which internet links will you use? Write the links here:
....
....
....
....
....
....

Which DVDs will you use? Write their titles here:
....
....

☆ Finding Clue Words about My State ☆

When we first read and learn new information, that information may be difficult to understand or to remember. But you have learned to use clue words to make understanding and remembering easier!

As you begin to read and learn exciting things about the state in which you live, remember to look for the "5 W" Clue Words, words that tell who, what, when, where, and why.

Assignment:

Using the research materials from your state capitol visit or other resources (encyclopedia; library or other books; internet links), find out about the ancient history of your state.

If you are using an encyclopedia or book, look for headings or chapters titled "Early History" or "Ancient History" of the state.

Links:
- https://www.factmonster.com/explore-all-fifty-us-states
- https://kids.nationalgeographic.com/geography/states
- https://www.ducksters.com/geography/us_states/

For your internet search box:
- prehistoric + name of state
- ancient history + name of state
- name of state + prehistory
- name of state + early history

When you find information that looks interesting, print it out to save and read off-line.

Read your selections about the early history of your state. What were the most interesting points to you? Which seemed the most important?

Pick one important event and, on the next page, write down the "5 W's" from that one selection. (If you need more room, you can write this in your binder.)

State Study

Who is mentioned in this selection about the state's early history?

....

....

....

(did) What is mentioned in this selection about the state's early history?

....

....

....

When did the event or events happen?

....

....

....

Where did the event or events happen?

....

....

....

Why did the events happen?

....

....

....

....

For fun and extra credit, can you find the "5 W's" on a second event?

Who is mentioned in this selection about the state's early history?

....
....
....

(did) What is mentioned in this selection about the state's early history?

....
....
....

When did the event or events happen?

....
....
....

Where did the event or events happen?

....
....
....

Why did the events happen?

....
....
....
....

State Study

"5 W's": Ready, Set, Write!

The following "5 W's" tell about the ancient history of Washington, D.C., our nation's capital.

Who: Algonquian and Piscataway Native Americans

(did) What: lived in what is now our nation's capital; hunted and fished

When: before European settlers arrived in 1608

Where: Washington, D.C.; Potomac River

Why: because of the good fishing, hunting, and food gathering

Now let's turn the "5 W's" into a few simple sentences. Notice that we can put the "5 W's" in any order that we like!

The land that is now Washington, D.C., was once home to the Algonquian and Piscataway Native American tribes. These tribes fished in the Potomac River and gathered and hunted food in the woods near what is now our nation's capital. Then, in 1608, Europeans arrived to settle alongside the native tribes.

Assignment:

Underline the word or words that tell "who" in the paragraph above. Write "who" under the information. Do the same with the rest of the "5 W's."

Now you are ready to write about your "5 W's," too. Use the information from your previous assignment on the "5 W's" to write 3-5 sentences telling *who, (did) what, where, when,* and *why* in the early history of your state. (Please write on a separate sheet of paper. Keep your paper in your 3-ring binder for later use.)

Mapping My State

Use your resources to trace an outline map of your state, or download a map using one of the links below. The map should be large enough to cover most of an 8 ½" x 11" sheet of paper. (Please enlarge it, if necessary.)

You will need three (3) copies for your state project, *so please make three copies now*.

Links:
>   https://www.netstate.com/—*Click on your state under "State Maps" (the column on the far left).*
>   https://www.factmonster.com/atlas/map-library

Now, *trace* your map on a blank sheet of paper. Tracing the map will help you learn the boundaries and features of your state.

When you have traced your map, mark the location of the three largest cities with a dot and the name of the city. Mark the location of the state capital with a star. Now draw a tiny house to show where you live.

Now look at a map of your state taken from your research materials. How many of the bodies of water, towns, and cities have Native American names?

When you finish your map, write at the top, "[Name of state]'s Important Cities." Please slip the map in one of your binder pockets until your next map assignment.

Early History, Exploration, and Settlement

State Study: Week Two

If I Had Lived in My State Long Ago . . .

. . . what would I have eaten? Centuries ago, there were no grocery stores, no restaurants, no stoves or refrigerators.

Without refrigeration, food can easily spoil; if you eat spoiled food, you can become sick and even die. If you had lived in your state more than five hundred years ago, what might you have eaten if there was no fresh food available?

Depending on your state, you might have dined on smoked fish; parched corn; dried deer, elk, or bear meat; dried berries; pemmican; and even popcorn! These foods were smoked or dried in the summer when food was plentiful, to keep over winter and to eat when people traveled. Foods prepared this way kept for long periods without refrigeration.

Grocery stores sell dried meat called jerky; they also sell smoked fish, dried berries, and even a type of parched corn sold in the snack section and labeled as a "nut" made from corn. Plan a meal featuring foods similar to these; you might even make a type of pemmican for the meal.

Making Pemmican

Pemmican is a mixture of powdered dried meat, mixed with a pure fat (such as lard). Sometimes dried, powdered berries were added to the mixture.

To make your own version of pemmican, break up 3/4 cup of jerky and put it in a blender or food processor. Blend until it is powdered. Then heat 1/4 cup lard or rendered bacon fat over low heat. When it is all melted, mix the fat and jerky together. When your pemmican has cooled, form it into balls the size of walnuts and eat! (Because we *do* have refrigerators now, please keep your leftovers in the refrigerator.)

☆ Exploration and Settlement ☆

Who were the first Europeans to explore your state? Did they come from Spain, England, France, the Netherlands, or yet another country? Who were the first to settle there? Use the research materials from your state capitol visit or other sources to find out!

For your internet search box:
- early pioneers + name of state
- early explorers + name of state
- name of state + early settlers
- name of state + early history

When you find information that looks interesting, print it out to save and read off-line.

Assignment: Read your selections about the exploration and settlement of your state. Who first explored the state? What was the name of the first settlement? Where was it located?

Who first explored the state?

....

....

Who were the first settlers?

....

....

What did the explorers find that was interesting?

....

....

State Study

(did) **What** did the settlers do that was interesting?

....
....
....
....

When was the state explored? *When* was it first settled?

....
....
....

Where did the explorers travel? Pay special attention to bodies of water, mountains, or places that are mentioned.

....
....
....

Where did the first settlers settle?

....
....
....

Exploration and Settlement: Events and Places

Turn to the previous assignment. On a separate piece of paper, write at least one sentence for each "W" that you found about the explorers. Then write at least one sentence for each "W" about the first settlers. Remember to save your work in your binder for later use.

Enrichment:

Do you have friends or relatives whose *ancestors* (grandparents, great-grandparents, great-great grandparents and so on) came to your state long ago? Are there families in your parish whose last names are also the names of streets or businesses in your town? (This can be an indication that their families have lived in the area for generations.)

If you have the opportunity, talk with them about their ancestors. When did they come to the area? How has the town changed since their ancestors first arrived?

These people became a part of the history of your area. They may have served God faithfully and with great courage to help to build your community and parish in ways that have blessed the generations that followed.

Did you know that you, too, will be part of the history of your state? In what ways do you think God might call you to serve with courage in the continuing development of your community and state?

More Events and Places

Did you know that you can visit some of the sites, or very places, about which you are learning? For example, if you live in Virginia, you might visit Colonial Williamsburg with its living history programs. Or if you live in Maine, you can see the first permanent European settlement in Maine, at Colonial Pemaquid State Historic Site.

Those who live in Alabama can walk the same paths trod by ancient Native Americans at their settlement in Moundville; in Nevada, explore the Hickison Petroglyph Recreation Area or the Toquima Caves near Austin, which have drawings left by early peoples.

Your state, too, has exciting historical sites that you may visit!

Using your resource materials, locate where the events written about in the "Exploration and Settlement: Events and Places" assignment happened. Make up symbols that represent the events, such as a log cabin for a settlement or a canoe for an explorer who traveled by water. Draw your symbol on the "Exploration and Settlement: Events and Places" assignment that was saved in your binder. Now mark the places with the symbols on your "Important Cities" state map.

Use the research materials from your state capitol visit or make an internet search to locate other sites that were important in the ancient history, exploration, or settlement of your state.

If you are using an encyclopedia, find your state and then look for "Places to Visit" or "Early History" for ideas. If you are using the internet, search:

- your state + historical sites
- your state + department of tourism
- your state + tourism
- your state + travel guide

If there are search boxes on tourism or travel websites, type in "history," or look for headings on the website related to history.

Enrichment:

Libraries generally offer a good variety of DVDs that feature the history, geography, and places of interest in individual states. Visit your public library and find the section where educational DVDs are located. Find DVDs that feature your state and browse the titles.

Check out a DVD about your state's history, sit back with a bowl of pemmican, and enjoy the presentation!

Discoveries from Exploration and Settlement

As your state was explored and settled, pioneers delighted in the discovery of trees, plants, and animals that they had never before seen. States were sometimes named in honor of the Native Americans who lived there, and state mottos chosen to mirror noble values. Do you know the state tree, flower, and bird of your state? Where did your state's name come from?

Research and read your materials to fill in the boxes and blanks, below.

Links:
- https://www.factmonster.com/explore-all-fifty-us-states
- https://awesomeamerica.com/
- https://kids.nationalgeographic.com/geography/states
- https://www.ducksters.com/geography/usgeography.php

My state's motto is:

....

....

My state's name came from:

....

....

On a separate piece of paper, draw your state flower, state bird, and state tree. Slip the completed drawings into your state binder to save.

State Study

Statehood

State Study: Week Three

See an encyclopedia, other research materials, or links to find the information below. List the information at the top of a separate piece of paper. Save the piece of paper in your binder for the next assignment.

Date that [name of your state] was admitted to the Union

[Name of your state]'s first governor

[Name of your state]'s song

Links:
https://www.factmonster.com/explore-all-fifty-us-states
https://kids.nationalgeographic.com/geography/states
https://www.ducksters.com/geography/usgeography.php

For fun:
Do you know the words to your state's song? Learn it and sing it to your family!

https://statesymbolsusa.org/categories/song
https://www.netstate.com/states/tables/state_songs.htm

My State's Flag and Seal

Using the links below, find out about the symbols on your state's flag and seal. Then answer the questions below on the piece of paper you saved from the previous assignment.

Links:
> https://www.netstate.com/states/tables/state_flags.htm—*Click on "Find out more..." in the column titled "About the flag" (the column on the far right).*
> https://statesymbolsusa.org/categories/state-flag
> https://www.netstate.com/state_seals.htm
> https://statesymbolsusa.org/categories/state-seal

List the symbols that appear on the flag, and tell what each represents. Why do you think these symbols were chosen?

List the symbols that appear on the state seal, and tell what each represents. Why do you think these symbols were chosen?

Drawing My State Flag

Now, draw your state flag on an 8 ½" x 11" piece of paper. Slip the completed flag into your state binder to save.

Catholic Foundations

Living and Giving the Faith

As you begin to study the Catholic foundations of your state, remember that the Catholics you will read about were real people, just like you.

If you had lived in New York about two hundred years ago, perhaps you might have known a devout Catholic, a slave named Pierre Toussaint. Even as a slave, Pierre lived his life for love of Jesus. He saw around him children who had no parents, so he started an orphanage! There were African-American children in his city who could not go to school, so Pierre began a school for these children.

If you had lived in California at the same time, Fr. Arroyo de la Cuesta might have been your parish priest! Fr. de la Cuesta helped build a mission at San Juan Bautista. At the mission, Native Americans learned skills that would improve their lives. Fr. de la Cuesta also wrote an important book that helped preserve the Mutsun language; he had learned at least seven different Native American languages so he could share the Faith that lived in his heart and soul.

Or perhaps you might have played with little Katharine, a girl who grew up in a wealthy family in Pennsylvania. When she was grown, she gladly gave up her worldly riches for a far greater Treasure. Katharine entered religious life and started missions and schools for poor children all across the United States. Loving Jesus, and giving all she had to serve Him in the poor, was St. Katharine Drexel's greatest happiness.

The selfless love of Venerable Pierre Toussaint, Fr. de la Cuesta, and St. Katharine Drexel forever changed the lives of those around them. What examples these faithful Catholics set for us!

Are you ready to find out about faithful Catholics who brought God's love to your state?

Catholic Foundations

Who were the first brave missionaries to visit your state? Where was the first Holy Mass celebrated? What is the oldest parish in your state?

Do you know in which diocese your parish is located? Because some states have more than one diocese, you may choose to research either the information about your state, or about your own diocese.

> **Link:**
> http://www.catholic-hierarchy.org/country/dus.html
>
> **For your internet search box:**
> diocese of [your diocese name] + history
> Roman Catholic Diocese of [your diocese name] + history

Who were the first missionaries to visit your state or diocese?

....

Who was the first bishop of your state or diocese?

....

When did the first priests or missionaries come to your state or diocese?

....

What is the name of the oldest parish in your state or diocese?

....

Where is the oldest parish in your state or diocese located?

....

Now take out your "Important Cities" map and mark the location of the oldest parish with a cross.

State Study

⭐ More Catholic Foundations ⭐

In your previous assignment, you discovered at least four interesting pieces of the Catholic history of your state. Did you notice some of the "5 W's" as you researched?

Using the information from your previous assignment, write a three- to five-sentence paragraph about the Catholic foundations of your state. Write this paragraph on a separate piece of notebook paper; save your writing in your binder.

If you'd like, you may start your paragraph with this "writing prompt":

Filled with love for Jesus Christ, Catholic priests and missionaries set out to serve His children in [name of your state]. The first missionaries.....

⭐ Field Trip and Pilgrimage! ⭐

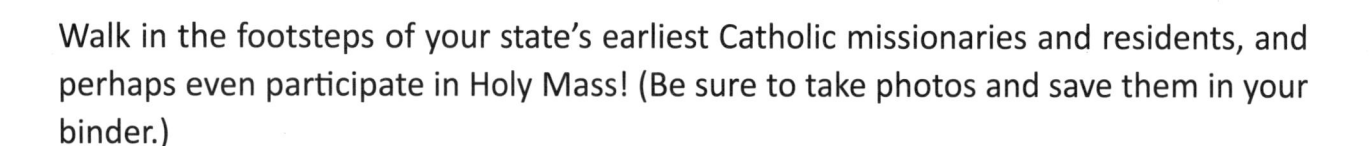

Walk in the footsteps of your state's earliest Catholic missionaries and residents, and perhaps even participate in Holy Mass! (Be sure to take photos and save them in your binder.)

> **Search:** "oldest Catholic church in [name of your state]"
>
> *OR:* go to your diocesan website to locate the oldest parish in your diocese
>
> *OR:* search shrines and pilgrimages by state:
>
> https://epicpew.com/100-catholic-pilgrimage-sites-in-united-states/
> https://catholicpilgrimagesites.wordpress.com/sites-by-state-2/
>
> If it is simply impossible to visit an old church or mission in your state, enjoy this tour of the California missions!
>
> https://missiontour.org/wp/

Geography, Climate, and Agriculture
State Study: Week Four

When you think of geography, your first thought may be of maps and countries. But geography can also include the study of a land's *terrain*. A region's terrain might be mountainous or flat, dry desert or damp rainforest, or grassy prairie. The terrain of a region can affect the types of *agricultural*, or farm, products that an area can produce.

The agricultural products of a state are also affected by *climate*, or weather patterns of that region. Fruits such as pineapple, oranges, and grapefruit grow in states that have warm climates all year round. States whose climate includes hot summers and freezing winters may instead produce wheat, corn, or soybeans as agricultural products.

Many states have more than one climate zone and terrain. That is, a state may have mountainous regions that experience cold, snowy winters, yet also have flatlands that are warm all year round.

If you farmed, which land do you think might be better for growing crops: flat land with soil that is easy to plow, or a mountainside with thin, rocky soil? Can you imagine trying to drive a tractor up a steep, rocky mountainside? How could a farmer possibly produce a crop in such a region? Just as importantly, how could such rocky land be used to produce food for a hungry world?

If you live in an area where vegetable crops can't be grown, but your state still produces quality food, I'll bet you know the secret. Animals can eat the grasses that grow where other plants cannot. Cattle are a food "crop," too! Do you live in an area where the terrain and climate simply cannot grow a vegetable crop, but where hard-working cattle ranchers nevertheless produce food to feed the world?

What do you know about your state's geography, climate, and agriculture?

My State's Climate, Geography, and Agriculture

See an encyclopedia, other research materials, or links to find the information below. Research and fill in the blanks.

Research Tip: Agriculture is often listed as a topic under the heading "Economy."

Link:
   https://www.netstate.com/—*Click on your state. See sidebar on left of page; click on "Economy" and "Geography."*

What is the climate of your state? Does it have more than one climate?
....

What is the average winter temperature in your area? Do you experience freezing winters? Write three or four words that describe your winter. (For example: cold, icy, snowy)
....
....

What is the average summer temperature in your area? Write three or four words that describe your summer. (For example: hot, rainy, humid)
....
....

What types of terrain are found in your state? Write three or more words that describe your state's terrain. (For example: rocky mountains, dry desert, grassy plains)

....

....

Think and answer: How do the climate and terrain help determine the agricultural products produced in your state? (For example, Hawaii's warm climate is perfect for growing pineapple, which cannot stand frost.)

....

....

What types of agricultural products are produced in your state? List at least three.

....

....

....

Sometimes states have nicknames associated with the products grown there. At other times, states have nicknames associated with their terrain or natural resources. What is your state's nickname?

My state's nickname: ....

State Study

☆ Agriculture and Natural Resources Map ☆

For this assignment you will use the second, unused outline map of your state that you made as you began this state study. (If you forgot to make three copies at that time, go to your state maps resource to make another copy.)

This week, you will draw small symbols or pictures of agricultural products produced in your state. Draw the symbols on the map where the products are produced. (For example, if cattle are raised in the southern part of your state, draw a tiny steer on that part of your map.) Gather your information by referring to your previous assignment.

Links:

https://www.britannica.com/—*type in your state and follow the links in the left sidebar*
https://kids.nationalgeographic.com/geography/states/

For your internet search box:

your state + agriculture
your state + natural resources

Next week you will use this same map to note natural resources, or valuable products that our Creator placed in your state long ago. (For example, trees and fish are natural resources.) Make your agricultural illustrations small enough that there will be room to add natural resources next week.

When you finish your map, write at the top, "[Name of state]'s Agriculture and Natural Resources." Please slip the map in one of your binder pockets until your next map assignment.

Writing about My State's Climate, Geography, and Agriculture

Using the information collected earlier this week, write at least two sentences *each* about your state's climate, geography, and agriculture. Also include one or two sentences that tell how the climate and geography help determine the agricultural products produced in your state. When you are done, you will have written an informative paragraph.

Be sure to use the words on pages 106-107 that you chose to describe the climate and terrain. These *descriptive* words add interest and detail to your writing.

An informative paragraph's first sentence *introduces* the topic, telling the reader what the paragraph will be about. The paragraph that you are writing will tell about the state's climate, geography, and agriculture, so those topics are included in the *introductory*, or first, sentence.

If you'd like, you may start your paragraph with this "writing prompt":

[Name of state]'s <u>climate</u> and <u>geography</u> in many ways determine the type of <u>agricultural</u> products produced by our state.

Write this paragraph on a separate piece of notebook paper; save your writing in your binder.

Create a "State Menu"

Prepare a meal that features your state's agricultural products. If possible, shop for ingredients at a farmer's market in your area.

If you live in Hawaii or Florida, you might prepare a fresh fruit salad. If you live in ranch country, you might grill a steak! If you live in a dairy state, your menu might feature a variety of cheese dishes.

State Study

Natural Resources

State Study: Week Five

You remember that natural resources are things found on and in the earth, not made by man, but rather created by God. Man uses these natural resources to meet his basic needs and more.

Nowadays, many think only of fish, wild animals, and water as natural resources. But natural resources include materials used in building and industry, and fuels. For example, trees from forests are cut into lumber; petroleum, natural gas, and coal are used to power vehicles and heat our homes. Just as important, these natural resources can power our industry and manufacturing, which you will learn about later.

Other natural resources include farmland; abundant water; fish; valuable minerals like iron, copper and silver; and stones like limestone and granite. Then, too, all of these resources are important to our states because they provide jobs for families.

Another "natural resource" that is often forgotten is *people*, the citizens of the state. Our loving Heavenly Father created and sent *people* with gifts to build up and serve others in hospitals and charities, working at home and away from home, to make a better life for all. Some of these people have become famous for their gifts, while others have lived lives of "hidden," heroic service to God and His beloved children. (Check your research materials to learn about a famous person from your state. Do you know of any other "human natural resources"? I'll bet you might even find some in your own home!)

Links:

https://www.ducksters.com/geography/usgeography.php—*Click on your state, then scroll down to find famous people.*

https://www.factmonster.com/explore-all-fifty-us-states—*Click on your state, then scroll to the bottom of the page to find famous people.*

My State's Natural Resources

What natural resources are found in your state? Do you know someone whose job is related to the natural resources in your state? See an encyclopedia, other research materials, or links to find the information below. Research and fill in the blanks.

Research Tip: You remember that a state's economy is made up of jobs and people who work in those jobs, and the money that is earned and spent because of those jobs. Because natural resources provide jobs, they are often found listed under the heading "Economy."

> **For your internet search box:**
> what are the natural resources of (name of your state)
> what are (name of your state)'s natural resources

List the natural resources of your state. If possible, also tell where each resource is found and how it is used. (For example: Sand, found in the southern part of the state, is used in the glass industry.)

Write at least one descriptive word to describe each natural resource.

Natural resource: ....
Location and use: ....
Descriptive word(s): ....

Natural resource: ....
Location and use: ....
Descriptive word(s): ....

Natural resource: ....
Location and use: ....
Descriptive word(s): ....

State Study

Natural resource: ....

Location and use: ....

Descriptive word(s): ....

Natural resource: ....

Location and use: ....

Descriptive word(s): ....

Natural resource: ....

Location and use: ....

Descriptive word(s): ....

Writing about My State's Natural Resources

Using the information collected earlier this week, write at least one sentence about each of your state's natural resources. Be sure to include your descriptive words in the sentences.

You remember that an informative paragraph's first sentence introduces the topic, telling the reader what the paragraph will be about. Your introductory sentence will mention each of your state's natural resources. The sentences that follow will tell a little bit more about each natural resource.

Write this paragraph on a separate piece of notebook paper; save your writing in your binder.

Agriculture and Natural Resources Map

On your Agriculture and Natural Resources map, draw small symbols or pictures of the natural resources found in your state. Draw the symbols on the map where the natural resources are found. (For example, one important natural resource of Alaska is fish, found both in the ocean and in rivers.) Gather your information by referring to your previous assignment.

Field Trip!

Take a field trip to see a natural resource, or something made from a natural resource.

Does your state have abundant water resources? If so, perhaps that water produces hydroelectric power through the use of a dam that you might visit. (Where water and dams are found, parks and picnic areas are often found as well. Take along a picnic lunch!)

Are fish a natural resource in your state? Visit a fish hatchery or cannery.

If your state is rich in clay, you might visit a brick or pottery factory. States rich in stone have mines, rock quarries, and gravel-crushing operations; those with prairie grasses have cattle and sometimes buffalo ranches!

Which natural resource "sites" can you find where you live?

Be sure to take photos and save them in your binder!

Industry and Manufacturing
State Study: Week Six

Industry and manufacturing both refer to work that uses natural resources or previously manufactured goods to make new products. For example, the paper industry uses a natural resource, trees, to make paper. The steel industry uses a natural resource, iron, to produce steel. That steel, in turn, is used to manufacture appliances, vehicles, and other products made from steel.

Just as important, industry and manufacturing provide jobs for citizens of your state!

See an encyclopedia, research materials that you have gathered, or links to find the information below. Research and fill in the blanks.

Link:
    https://www.britannica.com/—*type in your state and follow the links in the left sidebar*

For your internet search box:
    your state + industry
    your state + manufacturing

On the following page, list your state's industries. If an industry is related to a natural resource found in your state, tell which resource. (For example, a fish cannery uses the natural resource of fish, a granite quarry uses granite, and a paper mill uses forest products.)

If possible, tell where in the state the industry is found.

Type of industry: ....

Which natural resource the industry uses: ....

Where the industry is located: ....

Type of industry: ....

Which natural resource the industry uses: ....

Where the industry is located: ....

Type of industry: ....

Which natural resource the industry uses: ....

Where the industry is located: ....

Type of industry: ....

Which natural resource the industry uses: ....

Where the industry is located: ....

Type of industry: ....

Which natural resource the industry uses: ....

Where the industry is located: ....

Writing about My State's Manufacturing and Industry

Using the information collected earlier this week, write at least one sentence about each type of manufacturing and industry discovered in your previous assignment.

You remember that an informative paragraph's first sentence introduces the topic, telling the reader what the paragraph will be about. Your introductory sentence will mention each of your state's industries. The sentences that follow will tell a little bit more about each industry, from notes made in your previous assignment.

This week, after you have finished writing your informative sentences, you will add one more sentence to your paragraph. The sentence that ends your paragraph is called a *concluding sentence*. Concluding sentences are really easy to write, because they are almost exactly like the introductory sentence.

As the introductory sentence tells the reader what the paragraph will be about, the concluding sentence tells the reader what he has already read! The concluding sentence neatly "wraps up" your paragraph, giving it a final flourish.

Let's use the imaginary state of "Playland" as an example. Our introductory sentence might read, "Every child knows that Playland is famous for its manufacture of children's toys and playground equipment, particularly bicycles, train sets, and merry-go-rounds."

Because bicycles, train sets, and merry-go-rounds are the specific children's toys and playground equipment mentioned in the introductory sentence, we know that these topics will make up the "middle" sentences of the paragraph. Those "middle" sentences that provide detail might be written like this:

"Playland manufactures bicycles of every description, including tricycles, dirt bikes, bicycles built for two, and even unicycles. Smaller train sets made of wood are manufactured near Playland's southern forests, while larger sets made of metal are produced in factories in the port city of Shipsahoy. Merry-go-rounds have been manufactured for more than one hundred years in Faircity and Bigtop."

The concluding sentence of the paragraph might read, "The manufacture of children's toys and playground equipment, particularly bicycles, train sets, and merry-go-rounds makes Playland a state popular with children."

Notice that the concluding sentence uses almost exactly the same words, and repeats the same idea, as the introductory sentence. Simple, isn't it?

Now the paragraph is complete. It begins with an introductory sentence, has a sentence or two about each topic from the introductory sentence in its middle, and ends with a concluding sentence. Who knew that writing could be so easy?

Remember to write your paragraph on a separate piece of notebook paper; save your writing in your binder.

Field Trip!

Have you ever visited a factory where cheese, ice cream, or chocolate are made? How about a potato chip factory? Or a grain mill? You might be surprised at the factory tours available in your state. Use the link and search suggestions, below, or the research materials that you have gathered, to find factories that are open for tours. Many of the tours are free!

If the factory allows, be sure to take photos and save them in your binder.

Link:
> http://factorytoursusa.com

For your internet search box:
> name of state + factory tours
> name of state + industrial tours
> name of state + free industrial tours

When you are finished with your tour, add symbols that represent the factory and other symbols that are part of your state's industry to one of your maps.

Landmarks

State Study: Week Seven

Landmarks are places that have special geographic or historical significance. For example, famous South Dakota geographic landmarks include Mt. Rushmore and the Black Hills; a famous man-made landmark is the Corn Palace.

See an encyclopedia, other research materials, or links to find the information below. Research and fill in the blanks.

Link:
>http://www.collectics.com/museums.html

For your internet search box:
>name of state + famous landmarks
>landmarks + name of state

What are your state's most notable landmarks? Are they geographical features like volcanoes, or man-made landmarks?

....
....
....
....
....
....
....

What makes these landmarks famous?

....
....
....
....
....
....
....
....
....

☆ Topography and Landmarks Map ☆

Now you will create a third map, one which records the *topography,* or significant natural features such as mountains, deserts, rivers, and lakes. The map will also include famous man-made landmarks.

Draw small symbols or pictures of the topography and landmarks found in your state. Gather your information by referring to your previous assignment.

Famous People

You remember that people are natural resources, too. To each person He creates, God gives special talents and gifts. Some people, like Father Flanagan (Do you remember reading about him when you read about the State of Nebraska earlier?), use their gifts to help poor and needy men, women, and children. Others, like Thomas Edison (Do you remember reading about him, too?) are gifted in science or other skills and go on to create inventions that help improve people's lives.

Which people from your state do you think are the best "human natural resources"? Ask your teacher to read the list of people that you find, and together choose at least two famous people to research.

Links:

https://www.ducksters.com/geography/usgeography.php—*Click on your state, then scroll down to find famous people.*
https://www.factmonster.com/explore-all-fifty-us-states—*Click on your state, then scroll to the bottom of the page to find famous people.*

Person #1: Tell *who*.

....

What did this person do that made him or her famous?

....

....

....

When did this person live?

....

State Study

Why did this person do what he or she was famous for?

....

....

....

How (in what ways) did this person change society?

....

....

....

Person #2: Tell *who*.

....

What did this person do that made him or her famous?

....

....

....

When did this person live?

....

Why did this person do what he or she was famous for?

....

....

....

How (in what ways) did this person change society?

....

....

Writing about My State's Famous People

Using the information collected earlier this week, write a paragraph telling about the people discovered in your previous assignment. Remember to tell who, what, when, why, and how about each person.

Write this paragraph on a separate piece of notebook paper; save your writing in your binder.

Remember to begin the paragraph with an introductory sentence, follow with sentences that add details from your previous assignment, and end with a concluding sentence that repeats the information from the introductory sentence.

Field Trip!

How many interesting topographical features or landmarks did you find for your state? Did the famous people about whom you wrote have a part in creating one of the man-made landmarks? Or are there historical sites that mark the birthplaces or lives of the famous people?

Pick one of the sites you found, and visit! Be sure to take photos and save them in your binder.

Preparing My State Report

State Study: Week Eight

Did you know that this past seven weeks you have been writing a state report? It's true, and you're almost done!

Open your State Study binder. Notice that the information that you have gathered in your binder is organized by these topics:

- Early History, Exploration, and Settlement
- Statehood
- Catholic Foundations
- Geography, Climate, Agriculture
- Natural Resources
- Industry and Manufacturing
- Landmarks
- Famous People

In addition, your binder contains three maps that show the following:

- Important Cities and Places
- Agriculture and Natural Resources
- Topography and Landmarks

Your binder also contains drawings of your state flag, and photos of places that you visited.

Photos may be glued to sheets of heavy, three-hole punched paper and placed next to the categories they illustrate.

This week, you will organize your binder so that you can make an oral presentation based on the information in your report. When your teacher tells you that the information is arranged logically, you may begin practicing a presentation of your report.

Create a Cover

Of all that you learned about your state, what did you find to be the most significant? You may wish to design and create a cover for your binder, based on that most significant piece of information. Or perhaps you'd like to use your drawing of the state's flag, or a map, for your cover illustration.

Grand Finale
State Presentation and Cake!
State Study: Week Nine

This week's assignment is to make a "state cake" that will be served at the same time as you give your oral presentation. Invite family and friends so that you may share all that you have learned, and cake, too.

Bake a sheet cake, cut it in the shape of your state, frost, and decorate it. (Note: If you'd like, instead of baking a cake, you may use a recipe for crisp rice cereal bars. Instead of cutting into bars, this recipe may be patted out onto a cookie sheet, forming the shape of your state.)

Here are some ideas to get you started:

Mountain ranges can be created with chunks of cake and frosted white at the peaks; rivers and lakes may be frosted blue. Green-tinted coconut works well as grassland, with small plastic cows set out to graze. Mines might be represented with black licorice chunks for coal, or rock candies for minerals. If your state grows corn, candy corn may mark the map in agricultural areas. Mark the location of your state capital with a frosting star or a gumdrop. Use your imagination!

Have a party! Give your report as an oral presentation, using the features on your cake to illustrate your report topics. (Point out the geographical features as you give this part of your report; tell about natural resources and agriculture as you point out these features on your cake-map.)

You might like to print out copies of your state song, so you and your guests can sing it while the cake is cut.

(Before you serve the cake, take photos to add to your report binder!)

ANSWER KEY

TRICKS TO FINDING CLUES AS WE READ

P. 1 INTRODUCTION
1. c
2. b

P. 2 MORE TRICKS TO FINDING CLUES
1. Christopher Columbus
2. Niña, Pinta, Santa María
3. a.

P. 3 FINDING MORE CLUES
1. a
2. a
3. b
4. a
5. a
6. b
7. c
8. b

P. 5 WHY DID AMERICANS WANT A NEW GOVERNMENT?
1. ruled
2. country
3. colonists
4. list two: pay taxes on goods like tea; business taxes; couldn't say what they thought; couldn't meet freely in public; had to "board" British soldiers
5. Revolutionary War or American Revolution
6. from now on, America would be free of British rule

P. 6 AMERICA'S SYSTEM OF GOVERNMENT
1. freedom from Great Britain
2. July 4th
3. Constitution of the United States
4. b
5. c
6. the House of Representatives and the Senate
7. <u>judges</u> of the Supreme <u>Court</u>
8. a

P. 10 MATCHING CLUE WORDS: CONNECTICUT
1. The Fundamental Orders
2. Nathan Hale
3. Benedict Arnold
4. The Great Compromise
5. factories
6. Fr. Michael J. McGivney
7. transportation equipment; (list two) helicopters & airplanes, submarines, heavy machinery, scientific instruments
8. "under God"

P. 13 THE "FIVE W" CLUE WORDS, PART II
1. French and British

P. 8 A NATION OF IMMIGRANTS

2. started to fight or started to fight over the lands
3. 1750
4. northeastern America
5. Both the French and the British wanted the same land.
6. Answers will vary

P. 14 "DIG UP" THE CORRECT WORD: MAINE
1. Vikings
2. John Cabot
3. Massachusetts Bay Colony
4. Native Americans
5. Portland Head Light
6. Appalachians
7. ships
8. Fr. Sebastien Rale
9. respect

P. 15 MASSACHUSETTS: PILGRIMS AND PURITANS
1. Pilgrims
2. started the settlement of Plymouth
3. 1620
4. Plymouth, Massachusetts
5. Most of them weren't farmers... what they were used to in England.

P. 16 "DIG UP" THE CORRECT WORDS: MASSACHUSETTS
1. Plymouth
2. Massachusetts Bay Colony
3. Massasoit, Squanto, Samoset
4. Boston Massacre
5. Boston Tea Party
6. Paul Revere
7. Phillis Wheatley
8. She was a brave "spy," and homeschooled a man who became president: John Quincy Adams.

P. 17 MORE ABOUT MASSACHUSETTS
1. fish and other seafood
2. electrical equipment and computers and paper for dollar bills

3. b
4. b
5. a
6. b
7. c

P. 18 OTHER NEW ENGLAND STATES AND THE BILL OF RIGHTS
1. Vermont is landlocked; New Hampshire has only a small bit of coastline. The rest of the states are all close to the ocean.
2. b
3. a
4. b
5. b
6. a
7. c

P. 22 NEW ENGLAND REGION REVIEW/TEST
1. b
2. b
3. a
4. c
5. b
6. a
7. c
8. a
9. b
10. c
11. b
12. a
13. a
14. c
15. a
16. New Hampshire—Concord
17. Rhode Island—Providence
18. Vermont—Montpelier
19. Connecticut—Hartford
20. Maine—Augusta
21. Massachusetts—Boston

P. 28 THE MID-ATLANTIC REGION
1. Dutch and English (The Netherlands and Great Britain)
2. 16th and 17th centuries
3. Great Britain

4. Dutch or The Netherlands
5. New Netherland
6. canals
7. the Erie Canal
8. Statue of Liberty; Ellis Island
9. Isaac Jogues; René Goupil; Jean de Lalande; Kateri Tekakwitha, Frances Xavier Cabrini; Elizabeth Ann Seton
10. William Penn
11. c
12. a
13. c
14. b
15. c
16. John Neumann; Katharine Drexel
17. Thomas Edison

P. 34 WHAT HAVE YOU LEARNED?
1. because the new territory was north and west of the original colonies
2. Huron, Ontario, Michigan, Erie, Superior
3. American Indians
4. "...what shall we have to fear?"
5. a
6. c
7. b
8. c

P. 36 FAMILY NAMES FROM HISTORY
1. Millers ground grain into flour in grain mills.
2. Archers used bows to hunt, or as soldiers.
3. Fletchers made arrows, or the feather part of the arrow.
4. Pipers played music on flutes or similar instruments.
5. Coopers were barrel makers.
6. Smiths forged and crafted metal.
7. Glaziers were glass-makers or people who crafted windows.
8. Brewers made beer or other spirits.
9. Weavers were cloth-makers.

POSSIBLE EXTRA CREDIT NAMES FROM PHONE BOOK:
Barber, Bishop, Bowman, Butcher, Butler, Cartwright, Carpenter, Carver, Cook, Count, Duke, Fisher, Foreman, Forester, Gardener, Hatter, Herdman, Huntsman, King, Knight, Lord, Mason, Page, Potter, Prince, Sailor Or Saylor, Shepherd, Shipman, Tailor Or Taylor, Tanner, Thatcher, Tinker, Weaver, Woodsman

P. 38 NORTHEASTERN AND MIDWESTERN REGIONS REVIEW/TEST

1. New Netherland
2. Erie Canal
3. Kateri Tekakwitha
4. c
5. Jacques Marquette, Mississippi
6. Orville and Wilbur Wright
7. New York—Albany
8. New Jersey—Trenton
9. Pennsylvania—Harrisburg
10. Illinois—Springfield
11. Indiana—Indianapolis
12. Michigan—Lansing
13. Ohio—Columbus
14. Wisconsin—Madison

P. 42 MIDWESTERN REGION: WEST NORTH-CENTRAL

1. Missouri Compromise
2. Robert Fulton
3. Pony Express
4. Linda Brown
5. Rose Philippine Duchesne
6. Great Plains
7. Sacagawea
8. Louisiana Purchase
9. telegraph
10. Homestead Act of 1862
11. Lewis and Clark Expedition
12. Samuel Morse
13. Father Flanagan
14. segregation

P. 44 NORTHEASTERN AND MIDWESTERN REGIONS REVIEW/TEST

1. b
2. a
3. Huron, Ontario, Michigan, Erie, Superior
4. a
5. c
6. b
7. a
8. a
9. New York— Albany
10. New Jersey—Trenton
11. Pennsylvania—Harrisburg
12. Illinois—Springfield
13. Indiana—Indianapolis
14. Michigan—Lansing
15. Ohio—Columbus
16. Wisconsin—Madison
17. Iowa—Des Moines
18. Kansas—Topeka
19. Minnesota—St. Paul
20. Missouri—Jefferson City
21. Nebraska—Lincoln
22. North Dakota—Bismarck
23. South Dakota—Pierre

P. 49 THE SOUTHERN REGION

1. industry or factories; agriculture or farming
2. plantations
3. secede
4. the Confederacy or the Confederate States of America
5. Civil War
6. Abraham Lincoln
7. Reconstruction
8. slavery
9. Answers will vary. First, the country itself was torn into two parts. Lincoln was president of the Union; Mrs. Lincoln's brothers fought for the Confederacy. In some families, brothers fought against each other. Many, including Grant and Lee, had ties both with the North and the South.

P. 50 FLORIDA, MARYLAND, AND VIRGINIA

1. Ponce de León
2. St. Augustine
3. Everglades
4. George Calvert
5. Toleration Act of Maryland
6. Charles Carroll of Carrollton
7. The Star Spangled Banner
8. 1607
9. Jamestown
10. Pocahontas
11. Patrick Henry
12. George Washington
13. Thomas Jefferson
14. Robert E. Lee

P. 54 MORE SOUTH ATLANTIC STATES

1. cotton gin
2. slaves
3. Gen. William Sherman
4. Martin Luther King, Jr.
5. Carolina
6. the White House
7. Daniel Carroll
8. Fort Sumter
9. Abraham Lincoln
10. Washington, D.C.
11. District of Columbia
12. executive—president
legislative—Congress
judicial—Supreme Court

P. 60 THE EAST SOUTH-CENTRAL REGION

1. b
2. c
3. a
4. b
5. a
6. c
7. c
8. a
9. a
10. c

130

P. 62 THE WEST SOUTH-CENTRAL REGION
1. a
2. c
3. a
4. c
5. c
6. b
7. a
8. b

P. 64 THE SOUTHERN REGION REVIEW/TEST
1. plantations
2. c
3. Civil War
4. b
5. a
6. a
7. c
8. Washington, D.C.
9. a
10. the Dust Bowl
11. c
12. Delaware—Dover
13. Florida—Tallahassee
14. Georgia—Atlanta
15. Maryland—Annapolis
16. N. Carolina—Raleigh
17. S. Carolina—Columbia
18. Virginia—Richmond
19. West Virginia—Charleston
20. Alabama Montgomery
21. Kentucky—Frankfort
22. Mississippi—Jackson
23. Tennessee—Nashville
24. Arkansas—Little Rock
25. Louisiana—Baton Rouge
26. Oklahoma—Oklahoma City
27. Texas—Austin

P. 70 WESTERN REGION: MOUNTAIN
1. Mexican-American War
2. Sister Blandina Segale
3. cliff dwellings
4. Continental Divide
5. Sitting Bull, Crazy Horse
6. 13th
7. Transcontinental Railroad
8. Wyoming

P. 76 WESTERN REGION: PACIFIC
1. Russians
2. 1700s
3. gold
4. to find/dig for gold
5. Junipero Serra
6. Hawaii or Molokai
7. latitude
8. longitude
9. Northern Mariana Islands
American Samoa
Guam
U.S. Virgin Islands
Puerto Rico

P. 79 "5 W'S": MAKING SENSE AND SENTENCES
Answers will vary
Who: Senator Daniel Inoyue
(did)What: helped the wounded at the bombing of Pearl Harbor (student may also mention that he was a war hero and senator)
When: Pearl Harbor was bombed Dec. 7, 1941
Where: Pearl Harbor
Why: The Japanese bombed Pearl Harbor and the US entered WWII.

P. 80 WESTERN REGION REVIEW/TEST
1. Santa Fe Trail
2. c
3. Transcontinental Railroad
4. b
5. a
6. b
7. c
8. latitude
9. longitude
10. a
11. Alaska—Juneau
12. Arizona—Phoenix
13. Oregon—Salem
14. Nevada—Carson City
15. Washington—Olympia
16. Utah—Salt Lake City
17. Hawaii—Honolulu
18. New Mexico—Santa Fe
19. Idaho—Boise
20. California—Sacramento
21. Montana—Helena
22. Wyoming—Cheyenne
23. Colorado—Denver